> Do you really desire to be successful or do you simply desire the
> fruits of success? To achieve the fruits of success requires that
> you be committed to the whole of success.
> Success is indivisible. The fruit, which almost anyone would gladly
> accept, does not come separate from the effort, which far fewer are
> willing to embrace. Being successful means being committed to the
> entire process of success.
> That includes setting the goals, making the plans, putting forth the
> effort, and persistently working through the challenges until the
> desired results are a reality.
> Success is available to anyone who is willing to accept it in its
> entirety. It is as much effort as it is treasure. Indeed, the value
> of any success for you is equal to what you put into it. Do you really
> desire success, and all that it involves? Desire the whole of success
> and it is yours.
> Ralph Marston
>

How to Be an Up Person in a Down World DEVOTIONAL

Honor Books
Tulsa, Oklahoma

How to Be an Up Person in a Down World Devotional
ISBN 1-56292-459-1
Copyright © 1998 by **Honor Books, Inc.**
P.O. Box 55388
Tulsa, Oklahoma 74155

Manuscript prepared by W. B. Freeman Concepts, Inc., Tulsa, Oklahoma

References

Introduction

Where do you look when life tries to press you down?

- Someone else gets promoted

- You get a flat tire in a rainstorm

- One of the kids brings home a bad report card

- Not even your dog wants to be best friends any more

The place to look is up! Life is always brighter when we turn our eyes to the Giver of Light . . . the God who loves us and cares for our every need.

Discover how to build an unbeatable strategy for handling anything life throws your way with grace and poise.

Inspiring quotes, stories, and verses provide powerful words of insight and encouragement to help you live like an *Up Person in a Down World!*

**Yesterday is a canceled check;
tomorrow is a promissory note;
today is the only cash you have,
so spend it wisely.**

❁   ❁   ❁

Now is the acceptable time.

2 Corinthians 6:2 NRSV

"In a Chinese Garden," is the story of how a patient named Marguerite impacted the life of Dr. Frederic Loomis, an ob/gyn in China. The young woman had lost her baby and Dr. Loomis had gone to her bedside to grieve with her.

After her release from the hospital she wrote to him, recalling the fatigue she had seen in him and sharing with him a message she had seen on a garden wall. She hoped the words would be as meaningful to him as they had been to her: "Enjoy yourself. It is later than you think."

Her letter prompted Dr. Loomis to take a three-month leave of absence from his position at the hospital. He shared the letter with a friend, who spontaneously agreed to travel to South America with him.

In South America, they met a prominent man with whom they shared their story. The next day, this man told Dr. Loomis that he had decided to take his family for a long overdue vacation. He said, "It was a very long finger indeed that wrote those words on the garden wall in China."[1]

Through the years, countless others have responded to Dr. Loomis' story, deciding to no longer put off the things they've always wanted to do to make life more enjoyable. Today, perhaps the message from the Chinese garden is for *you*: *Enjoy yourself. It is later than you think!* ✪

Problems are only opportunities
in work clothes.

❂   ❂   ❂

But thou, O LORD, be merciful unto me,
and raise me up, that I may requite them.

Psalm 41:10 KJV

For years, railroad authorities dreamed of a rail crossing the Andes Mountains, perhaps following the course of the Rimac River. Engineers from around the world were called in to appraise the project and they all declared it to be impossible. Then, as a last resort, a Polish engineer named Ernest Malinowski was called.

Malinowski's reputation was well-known, but at the time he was called, he was sixty years old and no one wanted to impose such a rigorous task on a man his age. Malinowski, however, assured the representatives of the various countries involved that the job could be done, and he was hired to begin work on what was to be the highest railroad on earth.

Construction of the railroad posed both geographic and political challenges. The project required sixty-two tunnels and thirty bridges, one tunnel running 4,000 feet some 15,000 feet above sea level. On two occasions, revolutions in one or more countries held up construction. Once, Malinowski had to flee Peru and supervise the project while in exile. Still, nothing deterred this aging Pole from moving forward on the railway that was considered one of the wonders of the world when it was completed in 1880.

What problem are *you* using as an excuse today? Change your perspective. What opportunities can you see in the midst of your problems? Put on your work clothes and get busy! That's what an "up person" does! ✪

Neither a wise man nor a brave man lies down on the tracks of history to wait for the train of the future to run over him.

✿　　✿　　✿

Be careful then how you live, not as unwise people but as wise, making the most of the time, because the days are evil.

Ephesians 5:15-16 NRSV

In 1872, Andrew Carnegie met Henry Bessemer, a "crazy young Frenchman," who had discovered a method for burning impurities from iron and converting it into a metal of far greater elasticity and strength — steel. Carnegie leapt into one of his most important decisions, saying, "I must start with the manufacture of steel rails, and start at once!" Carnegie dreamed of a world with *steel* railways, bridges, buildings, and ships. Rather than iron, farm implements and factory instruments would also be made from steel.

A skeptical world smiled. One critic wrote, "This time the daredevil of a Scotchman's gone completely out of his mind!" The Bessemer process had been fraught with failure, but Carnegie's intuition told him the potential was greater than the risk. He later said, "It was not a task for timid men."

With a handful of partners, he organized Carnegie, McCandless and Company. The business managed to survive the depression of 1873 and even improved its mill for the orders that Carnegie felt were bound to come as a result of economic recovery. Therefore, he was the one man fully equipped to supply the demand when reconstruction began and steel began to be recognized as the building material of choice.

Wisdom and courage are a pair, and both work toward the future. Make the most of today and don't let the "down world" stop you! ✣

The good news is that the bad news can be turned into good news when you change your attitude!

✪   ✪   ✪

*"Because your heart was tender, and you humbled yourself before the L*ORD *. . . and you tore your clothes and wept before Me, I also have heard you,"* *says the L*ORD.

2 Kings 22:19 NKJV

Harold Russell, a paratrooper sergeant in World War II, lost his hands in a training camp accident. In the agonizing weeks that followed, he was overwhelmed by a sense of failure and defeat. He lost all will to live.

When the time came for him to be dismissed from the hospital, his major said to him, "There's one thing you ought to keep in mind, Russell. You are not crippled; you are merely handicapped." Russell looked up the two words in the dictionary.

Crippled meant "disabled, incapable of proper or effective action." Handicapped meant "any disadvantage or hindrance making success in an undertaking more difficult." More difficult, but not impossible!

Russell felt renewed hope! He began to concentrate on what he did have in life and began to set new goals.

Russell won the leading role for "The Best Years of Our Lives" and enjoyed a long career as a Hollywood star, winning two Academy Awards. He later wrote his autobiography, went on lecture tours, spoke on the radio, and used his talents and abilities to their fullest, inspiring others who were handicapped to refuse to see themselves as crippled.[2]

An "up person" chooses to focus on what they have, while the "down world" focuses on what they don't have.

Be thankful for the gifts and abilities you have and work hard to develop them. God will reward you. ✪

You cannot escape the responsibility of tomorrow by evading it today.

✿   ✿   ✿

Son of man, behold, they of the house of Israel say, The vision that he seeth is for many days to come, and he prophesieth of the times that are far off. Therefore say unto them, Thus saith the Lord GOD; There shall none of my words be prolonged any more, but the word which I have spoken shall be done, saith the Lord GOD.

Ezekiel 12:27-28 KJV

On a voyage from New York City to San Francisco, the steamship Central America sprang a leak. A nearby vessel, seeing her distress signal, bore down toward her. Believing the danger to be imminent, the captain of the rescue ship radioed to the steamship, "What is amiss?"

"We are in bad repair, and going down," came the reply from the Central America. "Lie by till morning!"

"Let me take your passengers on board NOW," signaled the would-be rescue ship captain.

It was night, however, and the captain of the Central America did not want to transfer his passengers in the dark, fearing that some might be lost in the confusion. Feeling confident that the ship would remain afloat for a few more hours, he signaled his reply, "Lie by till morning."

Once again the captain of the rescue ship called, "You had better let me take them now."

Again, the reply came, "Lie by till morning."

An hour and a half later, the lights of the Central America could no longer be seen. The ship had gone down. Everyone on board perished.

Accept help when you're in distress. Trust in God and don't let the fear of the unknown stop you. You can't be an "up person" if you're sinking! ✪

17

It is kind of fun to do the impossible.

✿　✿　✿

But He said, "The things impossible with men are possible with God."

Luke 18:27 NASB

Speaking to a joint session of Congress in May 1961, President John F. Kennedy gave this challenge: "I believe that this nation should commit itself to achieving the goal, before this decade is out, of landing a man on the moon and returning him safely to earth." But to reach this impossible-sounding goal, a major technology development program first had to be designed and put to work.

Apart from war time, America had never seen such a massive effort: Astronauts were trained and rockets, launch systems, and landing craft were built and tested. At times, the labor force numbered more than 400,000.

Rocket expert Wernher von Braun viewed the massive project this way, "When we wheel out one of the rockets to the launch pad, I find myself thinking of all those thousands of parts — and all built by the lowest bidder — and I pray that everyone has done his homework." Saturn V alone had 12 million working parts. A 0.1 percent failure rate meant 12,000 failures. The Apollo II mission to the moon, with astronauts Neil Armstrong, Buzz Aldrin, and Michael Collins, succeeded in meeting President Kennedy's goal with five months to spare.

Impossibly massive, complicated tasks become possible when you break them down into small parts, then believe and act as if they are possible. With God, anything's possible! ⚙

Give me a stock clerk with a goal, and I will give you a man who will make history. Give me a man without a goal, and I will give you a stock clerk.

✵ ✵ ✵

Hold fast what you have, that no one may take your crown.

Revelation 3:11 NKJV

At the Community Pride Food Stores in Richmond, Virginia, families of students who earn A's and B's on their report card receive a 10 percent discount. Customers get free checkups for cholesterol and blood-pressure. Senior citizens receive a 5 percent discount on Tuesdays. And teachers with high achievers win trips to the Bahamas.

Johnny Johnson, the store's owner, wants his employees and customers to live up to the name of his stores: *Community Pride.* All eight Community Pride stores are in urban neighborhoods that were abandoned by major supermarket chains.

When Johnson was only seven years old, he told his sister he was going to be a millionaire one day. He recalls, "In fifth grade, I was the only one with a briefcase." He began working as a night manager of a grocery store after college and rose through the ranks, learning every aspect of the grocery business along the way. He then borrowed money to begin his own chain.

He prides himself on big, clean stores with reasonable prices and fresh food. He walks the aisles of his stores daily, helping out where needed, greeting customers, and dealing with vendors. He aims at even greater growth.[3]

Do you have a goal today? ✪

People can succeed at almost anything for which they have unlimited enthusiasm.

✪   ✪   ✪

Then they returned, every man of Judah and Jerusalem, and Jehoshaphat in the forefront of them, to go again to Jerusalem with joy; for the LORD had made them to rejoice over their enemies.

2 Chronicles 20:27 KJV

When a person is determined, what can stop him?

Cripple him — and you have Sir Walter Scott.

Put him in a prison cell — and you have John Bunyan.

Bury him in the snow — and you have George Washington.

Have him born in abject poverty — and you have Abraham Lincoln.

Load him with bitter racial prejudice — and you have Disraeli.

Take away her sight and ability to hear — and you have Helen Keller.

Afflict him with asthma until he lies choking in his father's arms — and you have Theodore Roosevelt.

Put him in the grease pit of a locomotive roundhouse — and you have Walter Chrysler.

Make him a second fiddle in an obscure South American orchestra — and you have Toscanini.

Hardships do not make a person great. But by holding fast to enthusiasm and faith in the face of hardship, you can become great. ✪

Try not to become a man of success, but rather try to become a man of value.

❀   ❀   ❀

It's much better to be wise and sensible than to be rich.

Proverbs 16:16 CEV

Most Christians cannot imagine partaking of Communion and being given the bread but not the cup. That was the custom in Prague churches in the late 1300s when a young priest named Jan Hus began reading the writings of an English theologian, John Wycliffe.

Hus began to advocate translating the Bible into the Czech language and conducting services in Czech, not Latin. He also argued that all those present, not only the priest, should be given the "blood of Christ" during Communion.

For a time Hus' views were tolerated, but then the archbishop moved against him. Two hundred volumes of Wycliffe manuscripts were burned. Faced with his own martyrdom, Hus declared, "I, Jan Hus, fearing to offend God and to descend into perjury, and fearing also to betray the Truth . . . am not willing to recant." He was burned at the stake in July 1415.

A thirty-year rebellion ensued between the Hussites and the emperor's armies. The rebels lost the war but won one important concession in the process: in Hussite churches, priests were allowed to serve wine to the congregation during Communion services.[4]

The pursuit of the right values and truth will always lead to success in God's timing. ✪

Rule #1: Don't sweat the small stuff.
Rule #2: It's all small stuff.

✿ ✿ ✿

For our light and momentary troubles
are achieving for us an eternal glory that
far outweighs them all.

2 Corinthians 4:17

On his way home from a trip, a man stopped in at the general store. "It's great to be home," he said to the old-timer who ran the store. "Anything happen while I was away?"

Old Henry thought for a minute and finally said, "No, not really. Oh, your dog died."

The man cried, "My dog! What happened?"

"He got a hold of the burnt horseflesh."

"Burned horseflesh? Where'd he get that?"

"When your barn burned down, it killed your horses."

"How did my barn burn down?"

"A spark from the roof of your house probably flew over there."

"What happened to the house?"

"Oh, quite a fire. Sent sparks all over the area."

"How did it catch on fire?"

"Probably from the candles."

"What candles?"

"The ones around your mother-in-law's coffin."

"My mother-in-law's coffin! What caused her death?"

"Well, rumor has it that she had a heart attack when she heard that your wife ran away with the milkman. But other than that, there ain't no real news to tell."[5]

News is in the eye of the beholder, or the ear of the listener. ✪

27

Remember, no one can make you feel inferior without your consent.

✪   ✪   ✪

Haven't you read this scripture: "The stone the builders rejected has become the capstone; the Lord has done this, and it is marvelous in our eyes"?

Mark 12:10-11

Some people read the story of Elijah outrunning the chariot of King Ahab and raise their eyebrows in doubt. After all, the distance was about thirty miles and Elijah was not a young man, much less a marathon runner. (See 1 Kings 18:46.)

In 1865, however, a Maliseet Indian by the name of Peter Loler may have accomplished a similar but even greater feat. Loler was told by a stagecoach driver that he would not be allowed to ride the stage from Fredericton to Woodstock, New Brunswick, a distance of about sixty miles, because Loler was an Indian. Angered at this blatant display of prejudice, Loler vowed to get to Woodstock before the coach.

He raced ahead of the team of four horses, which had to be changed four times during the sixty-mile journey. Loler arrived in Woodstock five minutes ahead of the coach!

Never allow others to put you down in your own estimation. Refuse to accept their negative, demeaning criticism. Choose instead to prove them wrong — first, by continuing to believe in God and in yourself, and second, by giving your best effort to attain your own success.

Rather than curling up and hiding in rejection, an "up person" runs all the harder! ✪

Life is an echo.
What you send out — you get back.
What you give — you get.

❂   ❂   ❂

Whoever sows sparingly will also reap sparingly, and whoever sows generously will also reap generously.

2 Corinthians 9:6

An old-timer ran a feed store, but he just didn't seem to be able to make any money. The store's income kept creeping downhill until he feared he would have to close his doors for good. In desperation, he decided to pursue a "wild idea" that he came up with one night. He invested $50, a great deal of money in those days, in one thousand baby chicks.

His neighbors were quick to scoff. After all, this poor guy couldn't make it selling feed — how was he going to sell chickens? To their further amazement, however, the old-timer didn't even try to sell the chicks. He took a completely different strategy. During the months of February and March he ran an "Easter Special" — every customer received ten free chicks.

When word about this spread, the man's neighbors thought he'd gone completely mad. His feed business was about to fail and he was giving things away? By Easter, however, he was riding high. In fact, his business had tripled. Each of his customers who had received the free chicks were coming back again and again, it seems — to buy a lot more feed to nourish their growing brood![6]

Don't be afraid of giving. It's the first step to receiving! ✪

The key to everything is patience. You get the chicken by hatching the egg — not by smashing it.

✤   ✤   ✤

Therefore be patient, brethren, until the coming of the Lord. See how the farmer waits for the precious fruit of the earth, waiting patiently for it until it receives the early and latter rain.

James 5:7 NKJV

On the first Earth Day in 1970, David Brinkley was in England, in a beautiful little village complete with quaint homes with thatched roofs, green meadows full of sheep, and flowers of all types and colors. The road into the village was lined on both sides with great oak trees, some of which were reputed to be at least three hundred years old.

The County Council had recently told the village that the road into the town was too narrow for modern traffic and that it would have to be widened. To widen the road, however, they'd have to cut down the oak trees. There was no other possible route, given the general terrain of the area.

The village told the Council that they absolutely would not comply with the plan if it meant cutting down their trees. They argued and argued with the county officials until a compromise was reached: the county could proceed with its plan if it planted two new rows of trees thirty feet farther apart than the old ones, and only cut down the old trees and widen the road when the new trees reached the same size as the old ones — perhaps in two or three hundred years.[7]

The most valuable things in life always take time, but always prove to be worth it. ✪

Impossibilities vanish when a man and his God confront a mountain.

✪   ✪   ✪

I can do everything through him who gives me strength.

Philippians 4:13

Many consider "Ein Feste Burg" — "A Mighty Fortress" — to be Martin Luther's greatest hymn. Its majestic, thunderous proclamation of faith is a tremendous symbol of the Reformation.

Luther claimed that the hymn was inspired by Psalm 46. He became caught up in the patriotism which he found in the psalm, and attempted to reflect in his hymn the essence of an energetic, hope-filled faith.

This same psalm was also an inspiration to Sergius, a little-known hermit who lived in the fourteenth century. When Tartar hordes overran his land, Sergius turned to Psalm 46 for strength and courage. He recited the psalm over and over as he led his revived countrymen in a charge that drove back the enemy invaders.

What does Psalm 46 say? In part, it reads, "God is our refuge and strength, a very present help in trouble. Therefore we will not fear, even though the earth be removed, and though the mountains be carried into the midst of the sea; though its waters roar and be troubled, though the mountains shake with its swelling . . . the LORD of hosts is with us; the God of Jacob is our refuge" (vv. 1-3,7 NKJV).

Take courage. No problem is too big for God! ✪

You can make more friends in two months by becoming interested in other people than you can in two years of trying to get other people interested in you.

Love each other with brotherly affection and take delight in honoring each other.

Romans 12:10 TLB

Phil Connors, the fictional TV weatherman in "Groundhog Day," isn't interested in anyone but himself. "People are morons," he tells his producer, Rita, as they set out to cover the groundhog's finest hour. Why else, he reasons, would they make such a big deal out of such a silly holiday?

During his first Groundhog Day, Phil manages to belittle everyone he meets. He intends for his sarcasm to keep the Punxsutawney "hicks" at arm's length.

Everything changes, however, when Phil lives through the same Groundhog Day again . . . and again . . . and again. Because he has the "gift" of knowing exactly what will happen, he's able to play the hero: He buys a feast for a homeless man, catches a boy who falls from a tree, fixes a flat tire, uses the Heimlich maneuver to save a choking man, and convinces a nervous bride-to-be to go through with her wedding.

More importantly, Phil begins to treat Rita and his cameraman, Larry, with respect. By the end of the movie, Phil has a new attitude: he looks at people instead of past them.

Sarcasm and ridicule may get laughs, but they seldom make friends or create the progress that is born of friendship. When we turn our focus outward, to see the needs of those around us, we become a genuine "up person." ❂

Character may be manifested in the great moments, but it is made in the small ones.

✪ ✪ ✪

Well done, good and faithful servant! You have been faithful with a few things; I will put you in charge of many things.

Matthew 25:21

The whole world watched in awe as Shannon Miller captured the gold medal with a near-perfect balance beam performance at the 1996 Olympics. The moment was a monumental one both for her and for the nation — she was the first American to win both an individual and a team gold medal in a fully attended Olympics contest.

What most people fail to realize, of course, is that Miller's big moment was the culmination of thousands of lesser ones. Prior to that balance-beam performance, she had spent more than 20,000 hours in practice.

She routinely arrived at the gym by eight in the morning and worked out for four or five hours, returning again at three in the afternoon and working out another four hours — six days a week. Meanwhile, she managed to stay in school and keep up with her studies.

Her father and coach said of her Olympic performance, "The crowd sees the whole competition. . . . We see four events that we've been training for four years extremely hard . . . doing routines over and over."[8]

Don't be discouraged if it seems you're not accomplishing much. Remember, every little bit counts. Small accomplishments, minute by minute, day by day, eventually add up to large accomplishments.

Never discount any experience or any good effort in your life. God will count it as practice toward a greater achievement. ❂

Learn to laugh at your troubles and you'll never run out of things to laugh at.

❂   ❂   ❂

She is clothed with strength and dignity;
she can laugh at the days to come.

Proverbs 31:25

It takes sixty-four facial muscles to scowl, but only thirteen to smile. One elderly California woman may not have known that fact, but it certainly applies to her life.

During a very strong earthquake, eighty-year-old Mary Ann remained serene and unafraid. Some questioned her sanity and whether, perhaps, she was in denial or in the late stages of senility. Others conjectured that perhaps she had been through an earthquake before and that a former survival experience had led to her calm and hopeful demeanor. Still others felt that maybe, at her age, she simply had no fear of dying.

Mary Ann, however, offered this explanation when a reporter asked her, "Why weren't you afraid?"

"I never even thought about being afraid," she said. "I was too busy rejoicing at the truth that I serve a God Who is able to shake the whole world!"

To those who experience deep joy in God, difficult circumstances often yield more cause for rejoicing than reason to fear. Helen Keller once said, "Resolve to keep happy, and your joy shall form an invincible host against difficulty." ✪

**Between saying and doing
many a pair of shoes is worn out.**

✪   ✪   ✪

*You see that a person is justified by what
he does and not by faith alone.*

James 2:24

In 1932, a college junior sat in awe at the lectures of Sir Charles Singer, the celebrated British historian of medical science, and vowed to follow in his footsteps. He was crushed when his paper on the history of malaria was returned with the note, "Unread." To his surprise, however, he also found an invitation to have tea with Sir Charles.

During the occasion, he mustered the courage to ask why his paper had been rejected. Sir Charles said, "Perusal of your references made it clear that you had not read the original sources, and I have no time to review hand-me-downs."

"But it would be impossible for me to read Greek, Latin, French, Italian, and German," the young student replied.

Sir Charles shrugged his shoulders and said, "Why then did you not pick another subject?" The chastened student became an English major and put his scientific plans on hold.

Forty-four years later, however, he served as senior editor for *Tropical Medicine and Parasitology: Classic Investigations*, a collection of some two hundred original papers on parasitology translated from nine foreign languages. He gave ten years to the project.[9]

Luck may bring instant results, but it generally fades just as quickly. Genuine skill takes a lifetime to develop and use wisely, but it produces enduring excellence. ✪

A great deal of good can be done in the world if one is not too careful who gets the credit.

❂   ❂   ❂

When you give to the needy, do not let your left hand know what your right hand is doing, so that your giving may be in secret.

Matthew 6:3-4

One particular Sunday morning, the tenor soloist scheduled for a nine o'clock worship service got up on the wrong side of the bed. He experienced what singers often call "bad voice," not to mention the fact that he attempted to sing his song from memory, and his memory seemed to fail him as badly as his vocal cords did.

As he stumbled through the first verse of his song, people throughout the congregation began to pull their hymnals from the racks in front of them. They recognized the hymn as an old favorite, and they also recognized that their friend and brother in Christ was in trouble. As he began the second verse, his voice still faltering, the congregation joined in with him.

By the third verse, the tenor began to find his range. He seemed to take delight in leading the congregation as if it were his personal choir. By the fourth verse, the music truly was beautiful.

During the organ transition to the fifth and final verse the congregation fell silent, and the tenor went on to sing the most beautiful solo of his life.

God has called the body of Christ to help each other through hard times. When we work together, no one worries who will get the credit, because all the glory goes to God! ✪

Whether you think you can or you think you can't, you are right.

✹   ✹   ✹

Create in me a clean heart, O God;
and renew a right spirit within me.

Psalm 51:10 KJV

Years ago, new engineers in the lamp division of General Electric had to undergo a somewhat cruel initiation. They were assigned the impossible task of "frosting bulbs on the inside." As each struggling neophyte admitted failure at his attempt to complete the assigned task or acknowledged he was at a complete loss as to where to begin to tackle such a challenge, the other engineers enjoyed a good laugh at his expense and then welcomed the new engineer into their ranks with a good-humored handshake.

One day, however, Marvin Pipkin was the new engineer being initiated. He took his assignment seriously, without any idea that it was a joke. He went to work in his lab and refused to admit defeat even when his initial efforts failed.

In the end, he not only found a way to frost bulbs on the inside, but he developed an etching acid which created minutely rounded pits instead of sharp depressions — a process that actually strengthened each bulb when it was frosted!

No one had told Pipkin the job couldn't be done, so he did it.

You will never set a goal that is higher than your own beliefs about what you can achieve. First believe that a task can be done, and then make a plan to do it! ✪

If you keep saying that things are going to be bad, you have a chance of being a prophet.

❂　❂　❂

Son of man, what is this proverb you have in the land of Israel: "The days go by and every vision comes to nothing"?

Ezekiel 12:22

Sports psychologist and marathoner Jerry Lynch tells about a client, Paula, who arrived at a 10,000-meter run, looked about at her competition, and concluded, "There's no way I can win today. . . . I'm not good enough."

Two miles into the race, Paula was in the lead, but then she began to critique herself, saying, "I can't hold the lead. I don't deserve to be here." Her body tensed, her pace slowed dramatically, and she finished in seventh place. Later, she admitted that her negative self-talk led to her demise.

Lynch writes, "Harsh self-criticism simply sets you up to fail. It inhibits courage, confidence, and concentration, and creates tension, anxiety, and stress, which detract from efficient running. Keep constant check on your self-talk. Counter any negative 'chatter' with positive affirmations. Turn negative messages into positive ones. . . . Regular positive input will boost your confidence, make you feel better about your ability and direct you to higher performances."[10]

What is true for running track is also true for running the race of life. Believing you can is a prerequisite for believing you will; believing you will is a prerequisite for success. ✪

**It is never too late to be
what you might have been.**

❂   ❂   ❂

*Let the wicked forsake his way and
the evil man his thoughts. Let him turn to
the LORD, and he will have mercy on him,
and to our God, for he will freely pardon.*

Isaiah 55:7

He arrived at the University of Missouri journalism school with the lifelong goal of becoming a writer. Then his mother died and the war was on, so he entered the Air Corps. In need of cash, he returned home and became an insurance salesman. He worked hard but made very little money.

He was on a downward spiral, which left him in a pit: alcoholism, which resulted in the loss of his house, his wife and daughter, and his job. He was on his way to buy a gun and end his life when he found the book that changed his life, *Success Through a Positive Mental Attitude* by W. Clement Stone and Napoleon Hill.

He immediately applied to Stone's insurance company. He received good training and was soon the manager of a record-setting sales team. He wrote a manual about their success, *How to Sell Insurance to Rural People*, and Stone invited him to become editor of *Success Unlimited* magazine. A New York publisher read an article he had written for the magazine and offered to publish any book he decided to write. He jumped at the opportunity.

Within two years, Og Mandino's classic work, *The Greatest Salesman in the World*, was published. It has since been read by millions.

It's never too late to be what you've always wanted to be. Start now! ✪

The greatest use of life is to spend it for something that will outlast it.

Lay up for yourselves treasures in heaven, where neither moth nor rust doth corrupt, and where thieves do not break through nor steal.

Matthew 6:20 KJV

Joseph Ton, a former pastor in Oradea, Rumania, has written this about his experience as a Christian witness in an oppressive political climate:

"As I preached uninhibitedly, harassment and arrests came. One day during interrogation an officer threatened to kill me. Then I said, 'Sir, your supreme weapon is killing. My supreme weapon is dying. Sir, you know my sermons are all over the country on tapes now. If you kill me, I will be sprinkling them with my blood. Whoever listens to them after that will say, "I'd better listen. This man sealed it with his blood." They will speak ten times louder than before. So, go on and kill me. I win the supreme victory then.'"

The officer sent Ton home. He reflected, "That gave me pause. For years I was a Christian who was cautious because I wanted to survive. I had accepted all the restrictions the authorities put on me because I wanted to live. Now I wanted to die, and they wouldn't oblige. Now I could do whatever I wanted in Rumania. For years I wanted to save my life, and I was losing it. Now that I wanted to lose it, I was winning it."

When you discover something worth dying for, you discover something worth living for. ✸

**I don't know the secret to success,
but the key to failure is to try
to please everyone.**

❂   ❂   ❂

*No one can serve two masters; for either
he will hate the one and love the
other, or he will hold to one
and despise the other.*

Matthew 6:24 NASB

An old man once was walking with his son, who was still a boy, behind a donkey that they planned to sell at a county fair. Along the way, peasants reprimanded the old man because he was letting the donkey go without a load. "Donkeys are meant to carry a load," they said. Heeding their advice, the old man put his boy on the donkey and continued his journey. Then others who saw them censured the old man for letting his able-bodied son ride while he, feeble with age, walked. The man traded places with his son.

After they had gone a short distance further, they heard others calling to them, this time ridiculing the father for riding while his son followed like a servant. The man pulled the boy up behind him and they rode that way for awhile until still another group began to scold them for placing so great a burden on a donkey.

Having heard so many different opinions, the man finally stopped, tied the hooves of the donkey together, put a stick through them, and he and the boy carried the donkey. This caused still further criticism — and derisive laughter.

The father threw the donkey into a river and went home. ✪

**My obligation is to do the right thing.
The rest is in God's hands.**

✤   ✤   ✤

*You shall do what is right and good in
the sight of the LORD, that it may be well
with you, and that you may go in and
possess the good land of which the LORD
swore to your fathers.*

Deuteronomy 6:18 NKJV

When Al Sizer was only sixteen, his father died of a heart attack, forcing him and his mother into bankruptcy. Emotionally devastated, his mother had a nervous breakdown. Sizer vowed he would never let this happen to anyone else he loved.

He immediately began saving his money to buy a life insurance policy on himself, naming his mother as beneficiary. As soon as he was out of school, he entered the life insurance business with the intention that none of his clients would ever suffer as he had.

Sizer developed a clientele of more than five thousand people, for whom he wrote more than $51 million worth of life insurance. Several years ago, he contacted a man who told him that he didn't believe in life insurance. Sizer persisted and eventually talked him into a million-dollar policy.

Four months later, the man went for a walk with his brother. Feeling a little tired, he sat down on a park bench to rest, and a few seconds later, he died. Because of Sizer's persistence, the man's family is well taken care of and his business continues to flourish. He has said, "I know that I am fulfilling my purpose in life and what I do is important."[11]

There's no such thing as an unimportant career or job if it is one that serves others. ✪

**For all your days prepare,
and meet them ever alike:
when you are the anvil, bear —
when you are the hammer, strike.**

✪　✪　✪

*His lord said unto him, Well done, good
and faithful servant; thou hast been
faithful over a few things, I will make
thee ruler over many things: enter thou
into the joy of thy lord.*

Matthew 25:23 KJV

The story is told of Henry of Bavaria that at one point in his reign as king, he became very weary of court life and decided that he wanted to enter a monastery.

When King Henry presented himself to Prior Richard, the faithful prior carefully explained to him the strict rules of the monastery. The king listened intently and then expressed great pleasure at the prospect of such complete consecration to God.

The prior insisted that obedience to God and therefore, to him as God's representative — obedience that was implicit as well as outwardly expressed — was the first requisite if Henry was to be a monk under his authority. King Henry vowed to follow his directives completely.

Prior Richard then said, "Go back to your throne and do your duty in the station God assigned you."

The king took up his scepter, and from that day until the day he died, his people said of him, "King Henry has learned to govern by learning to obey."

Each of us is under the authority of someone, and ultimately, we are under the authority of God. We each were created for a specific purpose in His plan. When we choose to obey God and to fulfill His reason for our creation, we cannot help but succeed. ✪

Hating people is like burning down your own house to get rid of a rat.

❁   ❁   ❁

Whoever says, "I am in the light,"
while hating a brother or sister,
is still in the darkness.

1 John 2:9 NRSV

After his surrender in the Civil War, General Robert E. Lee mounted his horse and rode away, but not to his home. His home had been burned by Union soldiers. He felt great sadness, but no bitterness.

One Sunday at church he heard a preacher scathingly denounce the North. "Doctor," he said after the sermon, "I remember to have read in the Good Book that we must love our enemies." The astonished preacher said, "These words from you?"

"I have fought against the Union soldiers," the General replied. "But I have never cherished any vindictive feelings . . . I have never seen the day when I did not pray for them."

Although Lee held no animosity against the North, the North was far less forgiving. President Johnson had Lee disfranchised.

Eventually, Lee was appointed president of Washington College in Virginia, and there, at least, he enjoyed fulfillment in life. When he heard the mother of one of his students speak disparagingly of the North, he said to her, "Madam, don't bring up your sons to detest the United States. Remember that we form one country now. Let us abandon all these local animosities, and make our sons Americans."

No man is ever a loser if he can forgive his foe. ✷

**Some cause happiness
wherever they go;
others whenever they go.**

❂   ❂   ❂

*When it goes well with the righteous,
the city rejoices;
and when the wicked perish,
there is jubilation.*

Proverbs 11:10 NRSV

In *Out of the Blue*, Marlise Wabun Wind describes a visit she had with Sun Bear, a member of the Chippewa nation: "I asked Sun Bear for an interview when he came to New York, and . . . was surprised when he took me up on the offer. As I showed him around the city, he went everywhere with an unbelievable grin on his face. It made New Yorkers wonder if he'd just been released from an institution. In the city being unhappy is normal; being happy is considered crazy.

"Other people's attitudes toward his delight didn't bother him at all, but it embarrassed me to be going around with this grinning Indian. That made him smile even more.

"One day we got on the subway and he started beaming at everyone. One by one the passengers started smiling back. By the time we got to our destination, he had everyone on that subway car smiling. A subway full of smiling people was so incredible, it seemed a miracle."

Remember as you walk through your world today:

The world is like a mirror,
Reflecting what you do,
And if your face is smiling,
It smiles right back at you! ✪

The indispensable first step to getting the things you want out of life is this: decide what you want.

✪   ✪   ✪

When they had crossed [the Jordan], Elijah said to Elisha, "Tell me, what can I do for you before I am taken from you?" "Let me inherit a double portion of your spirit," Elisha replied.

2 Kings 2:9

James Post, M.D., makes his hospital rounds with an assistant who holds his stethoscope to the chests of his patients. Post's eyes, ears, and mind work excellently. His arms and legs, however, do not.

When he was fourteen, a diving accident at summer camp left Post paralyzed from the neck down. He completely lost the use of his legs and partial use of his arms. He kept his lifelong dream to be a doctor.

Post was rejected by ten medical schools although he finished in the top 10 percent of his college class as a pre-med major. Every school cited his disability as their reason for denying him admission. Finally, Albert Einstein College of Medicine accepted him, and he graduated in 1997. As part of the process, Post hired a physician's assistant to be his "hands" and his wife Saretha, did dissections under his instruction.

"The only surprise I ever saw was in some elderly patients," Post has said. "They would see a young, healthy guy in a wheelchair and say, 'Oh what happened to you, dear?' I would just tell them I was in an accident when I was young but I'm fine now."[12]

Decide what you want and where you want to go in life. When you're determined to get there, no limitation of any kind can stop you. ✪

What lies behind us and what lies before us are tiny matters compared to what lies within us.

The LORD does not see as mortals see; they look on the outward appearance, but the LORD looks on the heart.

1 Samuel 16:7 NRSV

Shortly after he lost the presidential election to Roosevelt, Alf Landon was invited to be a guest speaker before Washington's famed Gridiron Club. Governor Landon had carried only two small states in the election: Maine and Vermont. In his remarks, he chose to reflect upon his landmark loss with humor:

"A friend of mine wrote me recently that he doubted if my political experience had prepared me for the result of this election. I replied that he didn't know us Jayhawkers. If there is one state that prepares a man for anything, it is Kansas.

"The Kansas Tornado is an old story, but let me tell you of one. It swept away first the barn, then the outbuildings. Then it picked up the dwelling and scattered it all over the landscape. Both the farmer and his wife were knocked unconscious.

"As the funnel-shaped cloud went twisting its way out of sight, leaving nothing but splinters behind, the wife came to, to find her husband laughing. She angrily asked him, 'What are you laughing at, you darned old fool?'

"The husband replied, 'The completeness of it.'"[13]

Character on the inside, not circumstance on the outside, dictates one's ultimate fate! ✪

Promises may get friends but 'tis performance that keeps them.

❂　❂　❂

God is not a man, that he should lie, nor a son of man, that he should change his mind. Does he speak and then not act? Does he promise and not fulfill?

Numbers 23:19

Lord Palmerston, Queen Victoria's prime minister, was crossing Westminster Bridge one day when a little girl just ahead of him dropped a jug of milk. The ceramic jug broke into a thousand fragments, and she quickly dissolved into a thousand tears.

Palmerston was carrying no money with him, but he dried her eyes by telling her that if she would come back to the same spot the next day at precisely that hour, he would give her sufficient funds to pay for both the jug and the milk.

The following morning Palmerston was in the midst of an important cabinet meeting when he suddenly remembered his promise to the little girl. To the bewilderment of the ministers in the meeting, he jumped up, dashed out of the building, ran across the bridge, and dropped half a crown piece into the waiting child's hand.

He hurried back to his meeting, offering no explanation for his sudden "disappearing act" until the business at hand was completed.

Few stories are told of Palmerston's accomplishments as prime minister. But this one story of a promise kept has survived more than a century of retelling.

What promise do you need to keep today? ✪

Not everything that is faced can be changed, but nothing can be changed until it is faced.

✪ ✪ ✪

Confess your trespasses to one another,
and pray for one another,
that you may be healed.

James 5:16 NKJV

Mark, a New York architect, runs his own firm. Some years ago he experienced serious financial difficulties. He admits, "I felt like I was hearing the droning of the plane just before it crashed."

One day Mark ran into a fellow architect on the street. He asked Mark how things were going and in a moment of candor, Mark described the mistake he had made in pricing a job, an error that cost him all his profits. His friend said that he had made similar mistakes but had figured out how to correct them.

He told Mark in some detail how he did so. Mark said, "I stood there listening to the guy and realized I was getting about $100,000 in free advice."

As a result of that chance meeting, Mark put together an informal network of independent architects, which meets every few months. The rules are simple: all information, including financial information, is public. At each meeting everybody tells two stories, one success and one failure.[14]

Mark and his colleagues do what few people are willing to do: end the silence about failure in order to learn from it. The first step required to bounce back from any failure is to admit that you have failed, just don't wallow in it. ✪

There is little difference in people, but that little difference makes a big difference. The little difference is attitude. The big difference is whether it is positive or negative.

✿ ✿ ✿

*Happy is he that hath the God of Jacob
for his help, whose hope
is in the LORD his God.*

Psalm 146:5 KJV

The story is told of a king who suffered from a particularly painful ailment. He went to an advisor who told him the only cure was for him to find a contented man, ask for his shirt, and then wear it night and day. The king immediately dispatched messengers throughout his realm to seek out just such a man and to bring back his shirt.

Months passed, and after a thorough search of the kingdom the messengers returned — empty-handed.

"Do you mean to tell me that you could not find a single contented man in all my realm?" the king asked indignantly.

"O sire," the messengers replied, "we found such a man, but only one in all thy realm."

"Then why did you not bring back his shirt for me?" the king demanded.

"Master, the man *had* no shirt," they answered.

A person with a positive faith in God is content. The contented person gives generously because he has no worry about whether or not God will provide for him.

A giving person truly makes a difference. ✪

The Constitution of America only guarantees pursuit of happiness; you have to catch up with it yourself.

❂   ❂   ❂

Happy are those who trust in the Lord.

Proverbs 16:20 NRSV

In an article entitled "The Pursuit of Happiness," Jane Maxwell tells about one of her closest friends, Dory. Dory had worked for many years as a registered nurse and was looking forward to retirement. The year before retirement, however, she began having difficulty walking and often lost her balance. A CAT scan revealed the cause — an inoperable brain tumor.

Initially, both Dory and her husband, Bob, were devastated. Then Dory and Bob decided their faith was not based upon everything going as they had planned, but their faith was a decision to live in obedience to God and trust in Him, regardless of circumstances. They refused to allow cancer to steal their happiness.

Maxwell writes of Dory, "She has many friends visiting her; all go away uplifted in their own spirits." She concludes, "True happiness cannot be commanded to show up or forced to happen; it is not a condition, but an attitude. It is the difference between perceiving the negative trials that happen in our lives as hopeless 'Why me?' situations, or as challenging opportunities to learn, to grow, or sometimes just to be still and listen to our Father. It is our choice."[15]

What — or Who — is your source of happiness? ✿

I so desire to conduct the affairs of this administration that, if at the end, when I come to lay down the reins of power, I have lost every other friend on earth, I shall at least have one friend left, and that friend shall be down inside of me.

Search me, O God, and know my heart: try me, and know my thoughts.

Psalm 139:23 KJV

Michelangelo spent countless hours lying on his back, carefully painting the details of each figure on the lofty ceiling of the Sistine Chapel. The chapel frescoes are considered some of the foremost masterpieces in the world.

One day, a friend asked him why he took such pains with each figure, knowing that those figures would only be seen at a distance. "After all," the friend said, "who will know whether all of the details are precise? Who will care if the work is perfect or not?"

Michelangelo replied with a simple answer to both questions, "I will."

The only person who knows if you have truly done your best . . .

The only person who knows the real motives of your heart . . .

The only person who will ever know or remember everything you have done . . .

The only person who can fully appreciate your efforts and your attention to detail . . .

The only person who is thoroughly qualified to judge your performance . . .

. . . is you.

Stay true to who you are on the inside — that's where the "up person" is! ✪

Character is the ability to carry out a good resolution long after the excitement of the moment has passed.

✵   ✵   ✵

Then Gideon came to the Jordan and crossed over, he and the three hundred who were with him, exhausted and famished.

Judges 8:4 NRSV

During his record-setting, nonstop solo flight across the Atlantic, Charles Lindbergh recalls his own thoughts after having crossed the continent of North America, Newfoundland, three stretches of salt water, the first day, and the blackness of the first night: "I've let the plane veer off course again. If only those compasses would steady down, I could stop cramping my neck to see the stars, and rest. That's what I want most now — to rest. . . .

"If I keep the Spirit of St. Louis pointing generally eastward, that should be enough; that will bring me closer to Europe. . . . After the night has passed, I can hold a straight course. . . . I can't possibly miss the whole continent of Europe. . . .

"I shake myself violently, ashamed at my weakness, alarmed at my inability to overcome it. I never before understood the meaning of temptation, or how powerful one's desires can become. . . . I can't let anything as trifling as sleep ruin the flight I spent so many months in planning. . . . Honor alone demands that. The more my compasses swing, the more alert I must stay to compensate for their errors. If my plane can stay aloft, if my engine can keep on running, then so can I."

Endurance to finish is more meaningful than starting itself. ✪

**Laughter is a tranquilizer
with no side effects.**

✹   ✹   ✹

A cheerful heart is a good medicine.

Proverbs 17:22 NRSV

For years, comedienne Doris Roberts played the role of Angie's mother in the TV series "Angie". The story was about a mother who raised two daughters on the proceeds of a newsstand she owned. In one humorous episode, Roberts' character went to Atlantic City to gamble. It was an episode Roberts had great fun playing.

A few years after the program aired, she received a letter from a woman who wrote, "I hope this reaches you so you know how you changed my life. I had decided that I didn't want to live. You see, I had been diagnosed with multiple sclerosis, and had been sitting alone in a dark room, unwilling even to eat with my family or take any part in life. Then one day I saw you on Angie — the time you were going to Atlantic City — and I heard myself laugh out loud. It was the most amazing thing. I suddenly realized that if I can laugh, maybe there is some life left in me after all."

The woman went on to tell Roberts that she had ended her period of isolation and had gone back to college. Several years later, Roberts received a photo from this woman. The photo showed her in a graduation gown, having earned her degree cum laude.[16]

When you feel down, a hearty laugh is always the best medicine! ✪

Small deeds done are better than great deeds planned.

❂   ❂   ❂

Plans fail for lack of counsel,
but with many advisers they succeed.

Proverbs 15:22

An exhausted elderly couple entered a third-class hotel in Philadelphia one night. The man pleaded with the night clerk, "My wife and I have been all over the city looking for a place to stay. We did not know about the big conventions that are here. We're dead tired and it's after midnight. Please don't tell us you don't have a place where we can sleep."

The hotel had no vacancy, but the clerk took pity on the couple and offered them his own room, saying, "It's not as nice as the other rooms, but it's clean, and I'll be happy for you to be my guests for tonight."

The next morning at breakfast, the couple sent for the night clerk. He came to them quickly, with hopes that they had enjoyed a good night's sleep. The man then astounded the clerk by saying, "How would you like for me to build a big, beautiful, luxurious hotel in the city of New York and make you general manager?" Flabbergasted, the clerk stammered, "Wonderful!"

The guest introduced himself as John Jacob Astor. The Waldorf-Astoria was built — and the night clerk became one of the best-known hotel men in the world.

There are only two who know every kindness you perform — you and God. He is your Rewarder. ✪

Outside show is a poor substitute for inner worth.

✲ ✲ ✲

Woe to you, scribes and Pharisees, hypocrites! For you are like whitewashed tombs, which on the outside look beautiful, but inside they are full of the bones of the dead and all kinds of filth.

Matthew 23:27 NRSV

Suzie Humphries admits to having been full of herself as a television interviewer in Dallas. When she lost her job, she also lost her self-esteem. She had used all her money to buy the wardrobe she thought was important for her public image, so she suddenly found herself poor and depressed.

Then one day her phone rang, and a local radio station offered her a temporary job as a traffic reporter.

Desperate for work, she took the job. She showed up at the heliport at six o'clock the following Monday morning without even knowing how to operate the radio equipment or which direction the freeways moved.

That morning, she gave one of the craziest traffic reports ever heard in Dallas, but the people loved it. Soon, Humphries found herself making more money by working two hours a day on radio than she had working all day on TV.

Shortly thereafter she met and married her husband and soon gave birth to a son. She recently reflected, "I look back now and realize that if I hadn't been fired I'd still be sitting there on TV, missing the greatest gifts of my life. . . . You get knocked down, you come back up, better and stronger than ever, with gifts you never imagined."[17]

What others see on the outside is never as important as who you are on the inside. ✪

It is nothing against you to fall down flat, but to lie there — that's disgrace.

✪　　✪　　✪

My enemies, don't be glad because of my troubles! I may have fallen, but I will get up; I may be sitting in the dark but the Lord is my light.

Micah 7:8 CEV

Commentator David Brinkley has speculated on why President Bush became ill on his visit to Tokyo: "He left Washington, flew to Texas, hunted quail by day and ate barbecue by night. . . . Then a ten-hour flight to Hawaii, two miles of jogging before another nine hours to Australia and then into a boat to watch fireworks. In the morning, jogging again, shaking hands and signing autographs. Then to Canberra for ceremonies, back south to Melbourne, then back north to hot, steamy Singapore.

"A press conference in the tropical sun, two speeches, a visit to a school and a state dinner. Then to Seoul, South Korea, where it was freezing. To the tennis court. Next, breakfast with businessmen, meetings, a joint press conference, a speech to the National Assembly. . . . A visit to the American troops and back to Seoul for a state dinner. In Japan, from the Osaka airport by helicopter to Kyoto and some kind of game called *kemari*. Now a visit to the ancient throne room. . . . He opened a toy store, took a helicopter back to Osaka and then flew to Tokyo, where at dinner he passed out. Not surprising he passed out. It was surprising that he got up."[18]

There may be a good reason for falling, but there are few good reasons for staying there. ✪

**When one door of happiness closes,
another opens; but often we look
so long at the closed door
that we do not see the one
that has been opened for us.**

❂   ❂   ❂

*Looking unto Jesus the author and
finisher of our faith; who for the joy that
was set before him endured the cross,
despising the shame, and is set down at
the right hand of the throne of God.*

Hebrews 12:2 KJV

Christine never thought of herself as a doubting Thomas — until the death of her twelve-year-old son, Bobby. Two months after Bobby's death, she and her husband tried to escape their intense grief by taking a motorcycle trip from California to North Carolina. All across the Nevada desert, memories of previous trips taken with Bobby flooded Christine's mind and she found herself crying, "God, where are You?"

As she and her husband approached the state of Colorado, a strange feeling crept over her. Then, the thought came like a bolt of lightning: "We've never been to Colorado with Bobby. There are no memories here!" The closer they came to the Colorado state line, the more freedom she felt. Crossing the state line was more than entering new territory — it was a turning point in her grief.

Through the beauty of Colorado, Christine began to see that God still cared for her and that He had never left her. As they drove through the Colorado high country with its lush green meadows and brightly-colored wild flowers, she could once again thank God for filling her soul with His peace and her body with His strength.[19]

Is today the day to walk through a new door that God has prepared for you? ✪

Failure doesn't mean you are a failure . . . it just means you haven't succeeded yet.

❂ ❂ ❂

He who goes out weeping, carrying seed to sow, will return with songs of joy, carrying sheaves with him.

Psalm 126:6

It was August 1901. Wilbur had good cause to be discouraged. Their wingwarping system was unpredictable, and Lilenthal's data for computing the lift of their glider had been proven false. Wilbur later wrote, "When we looked at the time and money which we had expended and considered the progress made and the distance yet to go, we considered our experiments a failure. . . . I said to my brother Orville that man would not fly for fifty years."

Though discouraged, Wilbur and Orville did not give up. They returned to North Carolina's Kill Devil Hills in 1902 with their third glider and made almost a thousand glides. In 1903, they built their first flyer, a plane with an engine and a propeller, and achieved their first successful flights with it. A year later, Wilbur made the first complete circle ever flown in a plane. One year after that, the Wright brothers made what has been called "the first practical airplane," and by 1908, the first public flights were conducted by Wilbur in Le Mans, France.

In 1909, a Wright flyer was sold to the U.S. Army, the first-ever military plane.

Wilbur Wright told his brother that they wouldn't fly for fifty years, but it was less than eight. You may get discouraged, but don't quit. You may be far closer to the realization of your dream than even you think! ✪

A pessimist is one who makes difficulties of his opportunities; an optimist is one who makes opportunities of his difficulties.

❂   ❂   ❂

Then he who had received the one talent came and said, "Lord, I knew you to be a hard man, reaping where you have not sown, and gathering where you have not scattered seed. And I was afraid, and went and hid your talent in the ground."

Matthew 25:24-25 NKJV

Jeanne Marie arrived at Chicago's O'Hare Airport to discover that her flight to Pittsburgh was delayed three hours. Her gate was off the main corridor, so most of the seats were taken. Her mood went from bad to lousy. After about twenty minutes of angry pouting, she noticed a woman with a Crate & Barrel shopping bag take a seat next to a woman with a similar bag. They began comparing bargains.

"Twenty-five percent off," one woman said. "Thirty-three percent off!" said the other. She was annoyed at their congenial chatter.

Then a businessman said something and the women laughed. A man with a cane joined the conversation. A teen pulled off his earphones and listened in. An hour later, Jeanne Marie moved to take the seat next to the teen. The businessman asked, "Don't I know you from somewhere?"

They began comparing notes and swapping stories: forgotten luggage, major delays, missed connections, airport chair design. The loud snoring of a nearby man produced a gale of giggles. By the time their plane arrived, the new group of friends seemed reluctant to board. One of the women finally asked, "Do you think we should have a reunion?"[20]

One of the best ways to turn any negative situation around is to use the opportunity to make a friend. ❂

Joy is the feeling of grinning inside.

❂　❂　❂

For you shall go out with joy,
and be led out with peace.

Isaiah 55:12 NKJV

Two and a half years after artist Deneille Möes' mother became ill, she was finally diagnosed with Alzheimer's. As the disease progressed, Deneille watched as her mother's twenty-six grandchildren began to pull away from her and even Deneille found herself begin withdrawing emotionally.

During the Christmas season following the diagnosis, Deneille just rushed through the motions of celebration. Knowing her mother didn't have much time left, she felt no joy in the carols, gift wrapping, and baking that usually filled her with great excitement.

After her mother died the following April, Deneille felt she would never enjoy another holiday season again. The next December, however, when she stepped out into the season's first snowfall — bright and white and filled with promise — joy flooded her heart. She had an inexplicable desire to celebrate the love of God and strength of family that her mother had embodied. Her brothers and sisters felt it, too, and the entire family decided to go home to be with Deneille's father for the holidays.

As she lay awake that Christmas Eve, Deneille felt the assurance of Psalm 30:5 KJV — "Weeping may endure for a night, but joy cometh in the morning."[21]

Today, God desires for you to have His joy in your heart. ✪

**Even if you're on the right track,
you'll get run over if you just sit there.**

✪   ✪   ✪

March on, my soul, with might!

Judges 5:21 NRSV

In 1852, on a return voyage from England Gail Borden saw a need for spoil-proof milk. He noticed that babies were getting sick from the milk that came from the ship's two unhealthy cows. Back in the U.S., he threw all his energies into finding a solution.

First, he boiled the milk, but the product tasted burnt. Then he tried using vacuum pans, and over time he perfected the process. Even so, his patent application was refused for three years. When Borden finally opened a factory, he had to close it only months later because he was under-financed. A second factory was opened right in the middle of a nationwide financial panic. Borden, who used every opportunity possible to promote his product, happened to meet a New York banker on a train. He sold him on his idea and was able to arrange the loan he needed.

When the government made Borden's Eagle Brand Condensed Milk a part of the Union Army's field ration during the Civil War, Borden had yet another problem: keeping up with the demand!

When you pursue your God-given dreams with all your will, your dreams themselves will motivate you! ❂

**You see things and you say, "Why?"
I dream things that never were
and say, "Why not?"**

✦ ✦ ✦

*But as it is written, Eye hath not seen, nor
ear heard, neither have entered into the
heart of man, the things which God hath
prepared for them that love him.*

1 Corinthians 2:9 KJV

As A.H. Graenser sat in the lobby of a hotel in Omaha, things could not have been worse. He had just been locked out of his hotel room because he had not paid his rent. All of his baggage and his much needed overcoat were in the room. He had five cents.

As Graenser walked over to a lobby window, he noticed that the cold glass was steamed over from the moisture in the warm lobby air. He recalled that a chemist had once told him that if you rubbed glycerin soap, on glass and then wiped it off with a clean cloth, it would prevent such steaming.

Graenser spent his last nickel for a cake of glycerin soap at a nearby drugstore. Sitting on a park bench in the cold winter air, he cut the soap into twenty pieces and he thought of a name: Miracle-Rub. Then he began making the rounds of the city's filling stations, demonstrating Miracle-Rub on windshields. He sold his glycerin cubes for fifteen cents each, or $1.50 for a dozen.

He returned to the drug store again and again for more soap. By the day's end, he had twenty-seven dollars! He worked his way east and when he arrived in Detroit three months later, he had an automobile and a thousand dollars cash. There he founded the Presto Company, a prosperous firm that manufactured cleaning and polishing products.

God will always give you an answer — you just have to open your eyes and see the possibilities! ✪

Every tomorrow has two handles. You can take hold of the handle of anxiety or the handle of enthusiasm. Upon your choice so will be the day.

Never be lacking in zeal.

Romans 12:11

Orison Marden was born in 1850 in rugged, rural New Hampshire. At age three, he lost his mother; when he was seven, his father died. His guardian hastily sent him out as a hired boy. For the next decade, Orison hauled rocks, washed, and scrubbed for various families. He was regularly whipped, beaten, kicked, and nearly starved.

As a means of personal escape, he read, and one day he found a book in an attic that changed his life: *Self-Help*. The book told the stories of boys who had pulled themselves up by their bootstraps through energy, perseverance, and hard work. Marden resolved to become like them.

He became an entrepreneur, founding clubs and restaurants to put himself through college. He earned a law degree from Boston University and a M.D. from Harvard — simultaneously. He bought real estate on the side and by age thirty-two, he was very wealthy.

In 1897, he launched *Success* magazine, and in 1900, he moved his successful magazine enterprise to New York City. Dr. Orison Swett Marden was known among his 200 employees as a man who "filled everyone with his own enthusiasm and an urgent sense of the wonderful privileges and opportunities of life."[22]

Enthusiasm is the water that causes possibilities to grow into realities. ✪

**"One of these days"
is *none* of these days.**

✪   ✪   ✪

*A little sleep, a little slumber, a little
folding of the hands to rest — and poverty
will come on you like a bandit.*

Proverbs 6:10-11

Arnold Bennett dreamed of becoming a brilliant writer, although he saw no way out of his work as a poor clerk in a London law office. He determined, however, that time was the most valuable commodity he had, and he decided not to waste a minute of it. He budgeted each day's time carefully, allowing himself a margin of leisure time each day for writing. Soon, stories and articles began to pile up. Before long his first novel was published.

Arnold Bennett managed his time so well he also had time to pursue other interests: painting, music, theater, reading. People began to ask him, "Where do you find the time?" Bennett thought, *the key is not in finding, but in using.*

He then wrote the book, *How to Live on Twenty-Four Hours a Day*, in which he advised: "If one cannot arrange that an income of twenty-four hours a day shall exactly cover all proper items of expenditure, one does muddle one's whole life indefinitely. . . . We never shall have any more time. We have, and we have always had, all the time there is."

The idea of budgeting time like money was a new one, and the book was an immediate best-seller and remained so for many years.[23]

How you choose to live the next twenty-four hours is a good indication of how you are choosing to live your life. As you manage your time, you create your future. ✪

He that riseth late must trot all day.

❊   ❊   ❊

Let us get up early to the vineyards;
let us see if the vine flourish,
whether the tender grape appear,
and the pomegranates bud forth.

Song of Solomon 7:12 KJV

Cruising at 33,000 feet aboard a 130-passenger Eastern jet en route to New York, the captain and his first officer suddenly straightened in alarm — a rhythmic thumping seemed to come up through the floor. It was so distinct they could feel the vibration with their feet. They immediately checked all their instruments, but none of the warning indicators were lit. Thinking maybe the landing gear doors hadn't closed completely, they slowed the plane. Still, there was no decrease in the vibration. They began to worry about the engines. A check showed they were humming along perfectly.

The captain called ahead to New York to have a crew of expert mechanics ready to meet the plane when they landed. After they had safely landed the plane, the passengers had disembarked, and the mechanics climbed aboard, the senior flight attendant said to the captain, "We really had a weird passenger. He jogged in the lavatory next to the cockpit for twenty minutes. He said that he had slept in and missed his early morning jog, and this was his only opportunity to get back on schedule!"

The better way to get everything done that you want to accomplish in a day is usually to start early, rather than to plan to stay up late. ✪

**Business is like a wheelbarrow.
Nothing ever happens until
you start pushing.**

✿　　✿　　✿

*But Jesus said to him, "No one, after
putting his hand to the plow and looking
back, is fit for the kingdom of God."*

Luke 9:62 NASB

At age ten, Martha was fed up with earning fifty cents an hour as a baby sitter, so she started organizing children's birthday parties. Next, she worked as a teen model. In 1967, she joined a young Wall Street brokerage firm and through relentless effort, began pulling in a six-figure income.

By the early 1970s, Martha had tired of the rat race, but still enjoyed selling. She saw a void in the marketplace and pursued it, just as relentlessly as she had sold stocks. She put together a book about home entertaining and fought round after round with her publisher — who wanted to cut half the content, use half the photographs, and print only half of the 50,000 copies she believed would quickly sell. Martha continued to push forward, however, and proved that she was right. Her book, *Entertaining*, sold more than 500,000 copies between 1982 and 1997.

Throughout the next fifteen years, Martha produced eighteen more books, came up with an Emmy-Award-winning TV show, a syndicated newspaper column, a mail-order business, her own line of paint, and a successful magazine: *Martha Stewart Living*.[24]

A dream must always be yoked with persistent work if it is to plow a field that will produce a harvest. ✪

Our dignity is not in what we *do* but in who we *are*.

❂   ❂   ❂

What is man that you are mindful of him, the son of man that you care for him? You made him a little lower than the heavenly beings and crowned him with glory and honor.

Psalm 8:4-5

For several years, a group of one dozen black men and one dozen white men met once a month to discuss a question that arose from racial disturbance in their city: "Who are these people, and how can we know them?"

One day a black pastor made a comment to two white men about remaining patient. The statement seemed out of character to the men, who saw him as a make-it-happen kind of leader. He explained, "When I arrived at my first church, weeds had taken the place over, the building was in shambles. Five pastors had come and gone in three years. No one in the community had any confidence that I would be any different, so no one came to worship.

"My wife and I patched and painted and replaced the broken windows. . . . I decided to prepare and preach my sermons as if the place were full. . . . Finally, after three strained years, God gave us one family. . . . Slowly, over the next few months . . . God began to bless."[25]

Success had not produced this man's character, radiance, or leadership, as his friends had thought. His inner character and the decision to act like a leader had been what had led him to struggle and endure until he was successful.

A bearing of dignity always flows from inside out. ✿

**When you handle yourself,
use your head;
when you handle others,
use your heart.**

❂ ❂ ❂

*In response to all he has done for us,
let us outdo each other in being helpful
and kind to each other
and in doing good.*

Hebrews 10:24 TLB

During her three-year stint working at a women's resource center, Laurie Beth Jones had the opportunity to observe two very different leadership styles. The founder of the center treated every secretary and volunteer with the same warmth and respect that she did members of the board. She was truly grateful for the work everyone did and she not only knew the names of everyone in each staff member's family, but she took time to ask about each of them.

The leader who followed her had a much different style. She worked behind a closed door and communicated only through memos. She knew nothing about her employees' family situations. She barked orders, never lunched with any of the people she supervised, demanded overtime when extra projects poured in, and adopted a generally superior air. Productivity at the center plummeted.[26]

Part of the reason that Jesus' ministry was so successful was due to the fact that He met people where they were and accepted them for who they were. His respect created in them a desire to be better, try harder, and pursue what was right.

Today, treat others as the people they may well become: your eternal neighbor in heaven! ✪

In life, as in football, you won't go far unless you know where the goalposts are.

✵ ✵ ✵

Forgetting what is behind and straining toward what is ahead, I press on toward the goal to win the prize for which God has called me heavenward in Christ Jesus.

Philippians 3:13-14

As an infant, Brian Keith Weinstein struggled for every breath. At the age of six months, he was diagnosed with cystic fibrosis. Physicians told his parents that Brian was unlikely to live past the age of six.

Undeterred by this prognosis, the Weinsteins searched for a medical ally until they found Dr. Jack Gorvoy, who believed that with good care and advances in research, Brian might make it to his high school graduation. A regimen of antibiotics, supplemental enzymes, and a positive attitude in his family members produced a real turnaround in Brian's general health.

Brian's parents worked hard to bring him up as a normal boy. When CF kept him away from the track team and saxophone lessons, he turned his efforts toward a weight-lifting program and his dreams of becoming a physician just like his hero, Dr. Gorvoy.

Brian made the dean's list in college, in spite of a near-deadly bout with pneumothorax. He made it through medical school and began a five-year surgical residency at New York's Mount Sinai Medical Center in 1993. The pace has been grueling, but Brian has never been happier. Live only until age six? Not when you have a strong support group and a clear goal![27]

Are you in hot pursuit of God's goal for your life? ☻

Do not follow where the path may lead — go instead where there is no path and leave a trail.

✷   ✷   ✷

Enter by the narrow gate;
for wide is the gate and broad is the way
that leads to destruction,
and there are many who go in by it.

Matthew 7:13 NKJV

Norval Hawkins, the first Ford sales manager, always enjoyed telling the story of a car salesman in South Dakota who, in his words, was "too dumb to be afraid of tradition."

"Back in those days," Hawkins said, "people didn't drive cars in the winter. They put them up on jacks in the fall and they stayed there until spring. As a result, car dealers made no car sales during winter months. They virtually closed shop for half the year. But then, those at Ford's main plant discovered that one small dealer in South Dakota was sending them orders right through the winter." Hawkins was sent to investigate.

He discovered that the salesman sending in the orders was a "big, awkward, gangling, farmerlike youngster who confessed that he just didn't know he wasn't supposed to sell cars in the wintertime!"

His approach gave Hawkins an idea, and incentive. He persuaded his dealer organization to keep after-winter sales and to do whatever was necessary to make car-buying appealing during the holiday and post-holiday months. The result, in part due to Hawkins' insistence, is that January is now the peak month for auto sales.

Maybe it's time to rethink the approach you are taking in an attempt to resolve your problems. ✪

Whatever the majority of people is doing, under any given circumstance, if you do the exact opposite, you will probably never make another mistake as long as you live.

❂   ❂   ❂

Do not follow the crowd in doing wrong.

Exodus 23:2

When eight-year-old Christopher Harris got home from school on April 1, 1996, he watched clips of the Cincinnati Reds' opening day baseball game on TV. He was excited for his team's season to begin. But then, he watched as 51-year-old umpire John McSherry collapsed from a heart attack. McSherry died in front of 50,000 fans.

Chris watched with sadness and embarrassment as the Cincinnati fans booed when the game was canceled. He told his mother he wished the umpire's family knew that not everybody in Cincinnati felt the way the booing fans did.

The next day at school, Chris explained to his third-grade class what had happened. The children decided to help him counteract the tide of booing fans. They wrote and illustrated twenty-three hand-lettered sympathy cards, which eventually made their way to Marion Doyle, the umpire's longtime girlfriend. The cards arrived on what she called "a very tough day." Doyle, grateful for their thoughtfulness, arranged for the students to get tickets to a Reds game and be given a VIP tour of Riverfront Stadium.[28]

Never be afraid to swim against the tide of public opinion to do the right thing. ✪

The foolish man seeks happiness in the distance; the wise grows it under his feet.

✿　✿　✿

But seek first the kingdom of God and His righteousness, and all these things shall be added to you.

Matthew 6:33 NKJV

Fitness trainer Bob Greene was in one of his favorite places: Telluride, Colorado. As he overlooked the valley late in the day, he knew conditions could not be more perfect for skiing. The snow was a deep, fluffy powder. The air was crisp and fresh. Yet Greene found himself thinking: "I'm not happy."

In an effort to understand his feelings, he replayed the entire day, much of which had been spent skiing. Then it dawned on him. Virtually all day long, he had been somewhere else. He had been thinking about his career plans, buying a house, the day he was going home, and whether his car would start after sitting for two weeks. He said, "I was preoccupied with everything that I was going to do, and not anything that I was doing."

He began to reflect upon the last time he had truly appreciated any moment, and he realized it had been a long time. With this insight, he took off his skis and plopped himself down in the snow. He continued to stare at the mountains, but for the first time that day, he truly saw them. He soaked in their beauty. He forced himself into the moment. And he began to feel joy.[29]

Rather than focus on what you want, appreciate what you have. It may turn out to be enough! ✪

Dost thou love life? Then do not squander time, for that is the stuff life is made of.

✪　✪　✪

He also that is slothful in his work is brother to him that is a great waster.

Proverbs 18:9 KJV

The poem below captures well the fact that much of the way we choose to spend our time is drawn from our perspective on time itself. If we think we have a great deal of time, we tend to waste it. If we think time is short, we value every moment.

> When as a child I laughed and wept —
>> Time crept!
> When as a youth I dreamed and talked —
>> Time walked!
> When I became a full-grown man —
>> Time ran!
> Then as with the years I older grew —
>> Time flew!
> Soon I shall find as I travel on —
>> Time gone!

Ralph Waldo Emerson once had this to say about living each moment fully: "One of the illusions of life is that the present hour is not the critical, decisive hour. Write it on your heart that every day is the best day of the year. He only is rich who owns the day, and no one owns the day who allows it to be invaded with worry, fret, and anxiety. Finish every day, and be done with it. You have done what you could."

Life truly is an eternal today — make the most of it! ✪

Genius is one percent inspiration and ninety-nine percent perspiration.

✺ ✺ ✺

For you have need of endurance, so that when you have done the will of God, you may receive what was promised.

Hebrews 10:36 NASB

In 1895, a traveling salesman named King Camp Gillette had an inspiration that changed the face of man — literally. He said, "On one particular morning I started to shave and found my razor dull. It was not only dull but it was beyond the point of successful stropping and it needed honing, for which it must be taken to a barber.

"As I stood there with the razor in my hand . . . the Gillette razor was born. I saw it all in a moment, and in that moment many unvoiced questions were asked and answered more with the rapidity of a dream than by the slow process of reasoning."

Although he received the vision for his razor in but a moment, Gillette spent eleven years of experimentation and hard work before he saw his first dollar of profit. Along the way he spent more than $250,000 on lab tests to determine the quality of steel necessary. He experimented with blades for almost six years. He admitted, "If I had been technically trained, I would have quit."

In its first year of production, the Gillette company sold only fifty-one razors. By 1904, however, 91,000 razors were sold. By 1917, annual sales reached one million.

Your dream may have come in an instant, but it may take a lifetime to develop. Work on! ✪

That old law about "an eye for an eye" leaves everybody blind.

❋   ❋   ❋

*You have heard that it was said, "An eye
for an eye and a tooth for a tooth."
But I say to you, Do not resist an evildoer.
But if anyone strikes you
on the right cheek, turn the other also.*

Matthew 5:38-39 NRSV

A 17-year-old boy was viciously beaten with an iron pipe and stabbed a dozen times by two brothers who mistakenly blamed the young man for raping their sister. The victim's mother was devastated by the loss of her son, who had been her sole support. The woman had already suffered the death of her husband in an automobile accident and the death of a daughter to cancer. The entire community mourned the loss of this young man and was outraged at this violent act of revenge.

At their trial, the two murderers sobbed their apologies to the mother and their neighbors. To everyone's surprise, the mother publicly forgave them. She said, "Jesus died for my sins. He forgives me and expects me to forgive others. My grief is overwhelming, but I can bear to forgive these men."

Her remarkable display of faith impacted those around her with a force equal to that of the boys' violence.[30]

The greater the pain, the more difficult it is to forgive. Without forgiveness, the pain of loss is never released. ✪

Some people are always grumbling because roses have thorns; I am thankful that thorns have roses.

✥   ✥   ✥

Enter into his gates with thanksgiving,
and into his courts with praise:
be thankful unto him,
and bless his name.

Psalm 100:4 KJV

I saw him sitting in his door,
> trembling as old men do;

His house was old, his barn was old,
> and yet his eyes seemed new.
His eyes had seen three times my years,
> and kept a twinkle still,
Though they had looked at birth and death
> and three graves up a hill.
"I will sit with you," I said,
> "and you will make me wise;
Tell me how you have kept the joy
> still burning in your eyes."
Then, like an old-time orator,
> impressively he arose,
"I make the most of all that comes,
> and the least of all that goes."
The jingling rhythm of his words
> echoed as old songs do;
Yet this had kept his eyes alight
> till he was ninety-two.

— *Sunshine Magazine*

Your perspective on life is the number one thing that makes you an "up person." Be grateful for life and everything that comes — and goes. ✪

**I have noticed that
nothing I have *never* said
did me any harm.**

✦ ✦ ✦

*Let everyone be quick to listen,
slow to speak.*

James 1:19 NRSV

One day a harsh word, harshly said,
Upon an evil journey sped.
And like a sharp and cruel dart,
It pierced a fond and loving heart.

It turned a friend into a foe,
And everywhere brought pain and woe.
A kind word followed it one day,
Sped swiftly on its blessed way.

It healed the wound and soothed the pain,
And friends of old were friends again.
It made the hate and anger cease,
And everywhere brought joy and peace.

And yet the harsh word left a trace,
The kind word could not efface.
And though the heart its love regained,
It left a scar that long remained.

Friends can forgive but not forget,
Nor lose the sense of keen regret.
Oh, if we would but learn to know,
How swift and sure our words can go.

How we would weigh with utmost care,
Each thought before it reached the air.
And only speak the words that move,
Like white-winged messengers of love. ✪

How much pain have cost us the evils which have never happened!

❁   ❁   ❁

Be not afraid of sudden fear, neither of the desolation of the wicked, when it cometh.

Proverbs 3:25 KJV

Charles H. Spurgeon sometimes stopped in his pastoral rounds to talk to an old ploughman in the country. Although his words were often unrefined, Spurgeon found that he often spoke great wisdom.

In one conversation, the man said to Spurgeon: "The other day, sir, the devil was tempting me and I tried to answer him; but I found he was an old lawyer and understood the law a great deal better than I did, so I gave over and would not argue with him anymore."

"What was he tempting you about?" Spurgeon asked.

"I asked him, 'What do you trouble me for?' 'Why,' said he, 'about your soul.' 'Oh!' said I, 'that is no business of mine. I have given my soul over into the hand of Christ. I have transferred everything to Him. If you want an answer to your doubts and queries, you must apply to my Advocate.'"

Two of the enemy's foremost temptations are the temptation to worry about what might happen as a consequence of our past sin, and the temptation to believe that we have not been forgiven by God. These worries can be quickly resolved by pointing the devil to the Cross. Our lives and eternal souls are in the hands that were nailed to it. ✪

If you are all wrapped up in yourself, you are overdressed.

✿　✿　✿

For I say, through the grace given to me,
to everyone who is among you,
not to think of himself more highly
than he ought to think.

Romans 12:3 NKJV

A man who was involved in a ministry to university students once invited a prominent Christian speaker to address a group of students on his campus. When only one person showed up he refused to talk to her. He was too "big" to speak to a crowd that small.

Shortly thereafter, the disheartened campus minister was refreshed to hear the story of Edward Payson, a famous preacher of a former era.

One stormy Sunday, he had only one person in his audience. Payson preached his sermon as carefully and earnestly as though the building had been filled with eager listeners. Some months later, his lone attendee went to see him.

"I was led to the Savior through that service," he said. "For whenever you talked about sin and salvation, I glanced around to see to whom you referred, but since there was no one there but me, I had no alternative but to lay every word to my heart and conscience!"

As F. B. Meyer once observed, "The mighty great cares about the mighty small."[31]

When we yield the sin of pride to Christ's humility, we become more useful in His Kingdom. An "up person" esteems others more highly than himself. ✪

**No race can prosper till it learns
there is as much dignity in tilling a field
as in writing a poem.**

❁   ❁   ❁

*Whatever your hand finds to do,
do with your might.*

Ecclesiastes 9:10 NRSV

Every person has been gifted by God in some way. Furthermore, he has a destined time, place, and means of employing that gift so that it is effective for God's eternal purpose. Nobody else can fulfill another person's destiny — each person must fulfill his own. A gardener who loves to garden can make plants thrive when no one else can. A dog trainer who has a gift with animals can make even the most stubborn pooch behave. A short-order cook can juggle six meals at once when most cooks can barely prepare one.

Martin Luther King Jr. once said, "If a man is called to be a street sweeper, he should sweep streets even as Michelangelo painted, or Beethoven composed music, or Shakespeare wrote poetry. He should sweep streets so well that all the hosts of heaven and earth will pause to say, 'here lived a great street sweeper who did his job well.'"

Your gifts may be evident to others, or perhaps known only to you. Either way, never discount your gifts or think they are of little benefit to the world.

When you count your blessings, remember the unique gifts and talents God has given you. You have been "gifted" by the Supreme Gift Giver! ✪

It is a mistake to look too far ahead. Only one link of the chain of destiny can be handled at a time.

Therefore do not worry about tomorrow, for tomorrow will worry about itself. Each day has enough trouble of its own.

Matthew 6:34

The following poem, "Step by Step," by Barbara C. Ryberg, reminds us that if we claim to believe that our lives are in God's hands, then surely we must believe that each moment of our lives is included:

He does not lead me year by year
    Nor even day by day,
But step by step my path unfolds;
    My Lord directs my way.

Tomorrow's plans I do not know,
    I only know this minute;
But He will say, "This is the way,
    By faith now walk in it."

And I am glad that it is so,
    Today's enough to bear;
And when tomorrow comes, His grace
    Shall far exceed its care.

What need to worry then, or fret?
    The God Who gave His Son
Holds all my moments in His hand
    And gives them, one by one.

Be confident that God is with you every minute of every hour of every day of your life! ✪

There is no substitute for hard work.

So we continued the work . . .
from the first light of dawn
till the stars came out.

Nehemiah 4:21

Although he worked as a reporter for the New Yorker's "Talk of the Town" section, Charles Cooke's great love was the piano. He took advantage of his position to interview pianists such as Josef Hofmann, Artur Schnabel, and Vladimir Horowitz. He invariably grilled them for pointers, since he had purchased a Steinway B and had set aside one hour a day to practice. He wrote of his progress:

"Five years ago, I looked at the music of Chopin's B-minor Scherzo and was dismayed. I was convinced that it was hopelessly and forever beyond me. I kept on working. Today I play it." Cooke also learned Brahms' Rhapsody in G minor, Debussy's "Clair de Lune," Navarro's "Spanish Dance," and Schumann's "The Prophet Bird" — all considered very difficult pieces.

At the end of five years, practicing just one hour every day, he had memorized twenty-five compositions and was working on a new list of twenty-five. He said, "It is beside the point that I was born with little natural talent for the piano, and that my memory is a weak one which has to be bolstered with every memory aid I have been able to borrow or devise; we are talking about work here . . . tiring work, refreshing work."[32]

What might you accomplish by just working on it one hour a day? ✪

**Until you make peace
with who you are, you'll never be
content with what you have.**

✪ ✪ ✪

Godliness with contentment is great gain.

1 Timothy 6:6 KJV

Cleve Francis, M.D., is a practicing cardiologist and well-known country-western singer. At the age of twelve, however, he had no idea that he would be either.

About to embark on his teenage years, Cleve became keenly aware of the inequality of being poor and black. Though his family was religious, he began to wonder if God was punishing him for something.

One day, while walking with his mother on her daily seven-mile trip through steaming heat to the "big house" where she was a maid, he asked, "Mama, why am I black?"

His mother replied, "God is a good God. He made the heavens and the earth. He made the great mountains, rivers, and oceans. He made all living creatures and He made you. He gave you a beautiful black color. God made no mistakes, Cleve. You were put here on this earth for a purpose and you must find it."

Cleve was instantly filled with joy and a sense of purpose and belonging. And with this new perspective on life, he began seeking in earnest to find his purpose.[33]

God has created you with a specific purpose and plan. Have you discovered it? Are you living it? ✹

**Shallow men believe in luck . . .
Strong men believe
in cause and effect.**

❂　❂　❂

*You have all wisdom and do great and
mighty miracles; for your eyes are open to
all the ways of men, and you reward
everyone according to his life and deeds.*

Jeremiah 32:19 TLB

Ed Woods promised his son, Tiger, when he was only a toddler that he would teach him two things: course management and mental toughness. He has written: "One day, when Tiger was two, we were on the second hole at Navy Golf Course. He had hit his ball into the trees. 'What are you going to do, Tiger?' The boy replied, 'I can't hit the ball over these trees, Daddy, they're too tall.'

"'Well, what else could you do?' I asked.

"'I can hit it between those trees, but I've got to keep it down. And there's a big sand twap [sic].'

"'OK, what else can you do?' Tiger looked to the left and said, 'I can hit my ball out into the fairway, hit my next shot onto the green, and one-putt for a par.'

"I said, 'Son, that is course management.'"[34]

Tiger went on to manage not only courses, but tournaments. On Friday of the 1996 Walt Disney World/Orlando Classic, Tiger read the sports pages and then calmly announced, "Pop, got to shoot 63 today. That's what it will take to get into it." Pop replied, "So go do it." When he returned later in the day, Pop asked, "Whaddya shoot?" Tiger calmly replied, "Sixty-three."[35]

Some things we are supposed to think through and then make them happen. After all, God did give us a mind. ✪

Today well lived makes every yesterday a dream of happiness, and every tomorrow a vision of hope.

✿   ✿   ✿

Find rest, O my soul, in God alone;
my hope comes from him.

Psalm 62:5

A woman in a convalescent home was given a party to celebrate her one hundredth birthday. The media had been called, a large cake ordered, and invitations sent to the residents in each room. Relatives had come from several states. Streamers and balloons had transformed the home's cafeteria into a festive hall.

As the time drew near for the party to begin, the woman's pastor moved toward her to offer his congratulations just as a reporter also moved her way. Both suddenly laughed at something the woman had said.

A guest who observed this approached the pastor at the end of the party and asked what had happened to cause such laughter. The pastor explained, "Her mind was keen and alert. When I arrived, she was completely caught up in the excitement of the birthday party. A reporter had come to interview her. And when he asked that high-spirited, one-hundred-year-old woman, 'Do you have any children?' she replied without hesitation, 'Not yet!'"

Enjoy today to the fullest, and then expect to do the same tomorrow. ✲

There is no pit so deep that Jesus is not deeper still.

❂ ❂ ❂

Cast all your anxiety on him because he cares for you.

1 Peter 5:7

For some time, Perry Roll had carried a small aluminum cross in his pocket with GOD stamped on the crossbeam. The O was part of the phrase LOVES YOU imprinted on the vertical beam.

On a bus trip to visit his grandmother, Perry decided to get something to eat at Union Station's all-night restaurant. When a middle-aged woman sat down at the table across from his, he heard God speak in his spirit, "Give her your cross." Perry reached into his pocket and dug it out.

As he laid the cross on her table, he said, "God wants me to give you this." The woman read the inscription and began to cry. "Are you okay?" he asked. She nodded slowly and pulled her hand from her purse, along with a .25-caliber pistol.

"I came here to have my last cup of coffee," she said. "My daughter was killed a few months ago and my husband just left me. I thought God had abandoned me, too." Then she nodded at the gun and said, "Please take it away. I know I'm going to be all right." Clutching the cross to her chest, she walked out the door.[36]

We can never tell others often enough, "God loves you." Today, remember that "God loves you, too!" ✪

The spirit, the will to win, and the will to excel are the things that endure. These qualities are so much more important than the events that occur.

*It is good to be zealous
in a good thing always.*

Galatians 4:18 NKJV

As a sixteen-year-old Hungarian Jew in the Auschwitz death camp, Edith Eva Eger watched her world crumble around her. She saw her parents marched to the gas chambers. She was forced to dance for Dr. Josef Mengele, the "Angel of Death." She witnessed cannibalism and ate grass to stay alive, her weight dropping to 40 pounds. When the camp was liberated in 1945, an American soldier saw her hand move in a stack of lifeless bodies and pulled her out.

Today, she is Dr. Eger, a psychologist and assistant professor of psychiatry at the University of California in San Diego Medical School. She has said, "No matter what kind of situation a person is in, we all have inner resources to conquer it. I teach people that when nothing comes from the outside, you can get it from the inside."

At Auschwitz, she "never saw the world the way it was. I saw the world the way it could be. I developed my inner resources . . . something that no Nazi could rob from me. I made a choice to control my situation rather than let it control me."

The meaning of anything that happens to you is not embodied in the event; we give our own meaning to circumstances and situations. When you face difficulties, choose to bestow meaning that is endued with faith and hope. ✪

**Nobody has ever expected me
to be President.**

✪   ✪   ✪

*The noble man devises noble plans;
and by noble plans he stands.*

Isaiah 32:8 NASB

On his first day after being appointed the new president of Godfather's Pizza, Herman Cain met his executive vice president of corporate support, Ron Gartlan, and his new executive assistant. Then Cain wandered over to the employee lunchroom. Only one other person was there. "Are you new here?" she asked.

"Yes, I'm Herman Cain. This is my first day."

The woman responded, "Hi, I'm Lori. I work in accounts receivable. What do you do?"

Cain replied, "I'm the new president."

"I've heard every line in the book," Lori said, "but that's a new one." They both laughed, and then she said, "It was nice meeting you. I've got to get back to work. See you around."

That afternoon Gartlan called a meeting to introduce Cain to the staff. As Cain began to speak, he noticed someone sitting in the last row, trying not to be seen. "Hi, Lori," he said, and then explained to the group what had happened. Before the meeting was over, even Lori was laughing.[37]

Never underestimate a person's potential. In all likelihood, they are not yet who they are going to be. And neither are you! ✪

Hope is the feeling you have that the feeling you have isn't permanent.

❁   ❁   ❁

We also boast in our sufferings, knowing that suffering produces endurance, and endurance produces character, and character produces hope, and hope does not disappoint us, because God's love has been poured into our hearts.

Romans 5:3-5 NRSV

For years, Jim Stovall had been gradually losing his eyesight. Then, the day came when he awoke to total blackness. For the next several months, he spent most of his days in one room in his home — with a phone, computer, stereo, and other gadgets. Four walls. No hope. He said, "I started to get tired of that. One day, I walked out to the mailbox." It was only a few steps, but Stovall calls it the defining moment of his life.

Not many days later, Stovall met Kathy Harper at a meeting of blind people. Although legally blind, Harper still had some vision. Her background was in law. His was in finance. Although the two were very different, they shared a love for movies and television programming. Out of their friendship grew the idea for the Emmy-Award-winning Narrative Television Network — which airs programs that have an enhanced audio track which details the action and key features of a film or TV program.

Stovall has said, "Being blind is not the worst thing that can happen to you. Losing hope is." No longer in a single room — wired to the world but not connected to it — Stovall travels widely as a businessman and motivational speaker.

Never give up hope! ✪

He who receives a good turn should never forget it; he who does one should never remember it.

❀   ❀   ❀

The desire of a man is his kindness.

Proverbs 19:22 KJV

Forget the kindness that you do,
As soon as you have done it;
Forget the praise that falls on you,
The moment you have won it.

Forget the slander that you hear,
Before you can repeat it;
Forget each slight, each spite, each sneer,
Wherever you may meet it.

Remember every kindness done,
To you, whate'er its measure;
Remember every promise made,
And keep it to the letter;
Remember those who lend you aid,
And be a grateful debtor.

Remember good, remember truth,
Remember heaven's above you,
And you will find through age and youth,
True joy and hearts to love you!

We each have a "selective memory." The trick is to use our memory to remember those things that are good and God-given, and to ignore and forget those things which are not. ✪

**Destiny is not a matter of chance,
it is a matter of choice.
It is not a thing to be waited for;
it is a thing to be achieved.**

✪　　✪　　✪

*I have not yet reached my goal, and
I am not perfect. But Christ has taken
hold of me. So I keep on running and
struggling to take hold of the prize.*

Philippians 3:12 CEV

Motivated by the opinion that the South's economy needed diversification, George Washington Carver turned his attention to the sweet potato. He developed more than one hundred products from it, but none were as marketable as cotton. Then he examined the pecan, without success.

Years later, he was fond of relating to his students how he began his experiments with the peanut, at the time considered to be a worthless plant:

"I went into my laboratory and said, 'Dear Creator, please tell me what the universe was made for.' And the Creator declared, 'You want to know too much for such a little mind. Ask for something your size.'

"Then I asked, 'Dear Creator, tell me what man was made for.' Again the great Creator answered, 'Little one, you are still asking too much. Make your request a more proportionate one.' 'Tell me then, Creator, what the peanut was made for.'

"Then the great Creator taught me how to take the peanut apart and put it together again. And out of this came all these products which the Creator taught me to make."

In all, Carver wrested more than 300 products from the peanut and gave the South a new high-yielding industry.

God is waiting to show you your destiny. All you have to do is ask! ❂

Experience is the name everyone gives to their mistakes.

✿ ✿ ✿

Who can discern his errors?
Forgive my hidden faults.

Psalm 19:12

One day a young boy was carried, arms and legs flailing, into Dr. B.H. Kean's examination room, where the boy proceeded to emit a series of earsplitting screams. The child was a familiar figure at the hospital. His overly-protective, doting father had turned him into a confirmed hypochondriac. The medical staff at the hospital was weary of his many appearances at the hospital.

While three nurses pinned the boy down, Dr. Kean discovered he had a minor fever and the faintest signs of a sore throat. He said, "Give him an aspirin, and I'll be back after dinner."

The boy shouted, "I don't want aspirin! I can't take it! You can't make me!"

The doctor said, "Shove it down his throat, and I'll be back."

Minutes later, Kean was paged at the dining room and was told by a distraught nurse, "The colonel's son is dead!" Kean raced to the child's bedside, where artificial respiration, oxygen, and adrenaline injections revived the child. As he batted his eyes, he said, "I told you not to give me aspirin. I'm allergic to it."

In the wake of this incident, Kean adopted a policy of asking his patients, "What do you think is the matter with you?" Not infrequently, he notes, the patient is right.[38]

Part of learning from one's mistakes includes listening closely to what others say about them. ✪

Happiness is a direction, not a place.

✪   ✪   ✪

Thus says the Lord: Stand at the crossroads, and look, and ask for the ancient paths, where the good way lies; and walk in it, and find rest for your souls.

Jeremiah 6:16 NRSV

There once was an old, wise man who sat every day in his rocker outside a gas station, greeting those who passed through his small town. His granddaughter often sat at the foot of his chair to pass time with him.

One day a tourist asked, "So what kind of town is this?" The old man said, "What kind of town are you from?" The tourist replied, "In my town, everyone is critical of one other. The neighbors all gossip. It's a negative place." The old man said, "You know, that's just how this town is."

An hour later, another man asked, "Is this town a pretty good place to live?" The old man replied, "What about the town you are from? How is it?" The man said, "In my town everyone is very close and always willing to lend their neighbor a helping hand. There's always a hello and thank-you everywhere you go." The old man said, "That's a lot like this small town."

After the family had driven away, the granddaughter asked, "Grandpa, why did you tell the first man our town was a terrible place and the second man a wonderful place?" The old man smiled and said, "No matter where you go, you take your attitude with you and that's what makes a place terrible or wonderful."[39]

How is it where you live, work, and worship? ✪

The miracle is this . . . the more we share, the more we have.

❊   ❊   ❊

You will be enriched in every way for your great generosity, which will produce thanksgiving to God through us.

2 Corinthians 9:11 NRSV

One day while he was out for a long walk, Sam Foss suddenly realized how hot and tired he was. He saw a big tree at the side of the road and stopped to rest in its shade. He noticed a little sign on the tree that said, "There is a good spring inside the fence. Come and drink if you are thirsty."

Foss climbed over the fence, found the spring, and gratefully drank his fill of cool water. Then he noticed a bench near the spring. The sign tacked to it said, "Sit down and rest awhile if you are tired." As he sat down to rest, Foss noticed a barrel of apples nearby, also with a sign: "If you like apples, just help yourself." He chose a plump red apple and then looked up in surprise to see an elderly man watching him.

"Is this your place?" Foss asked.

"Yes," the old man said. "Glad you stopped by."

Foss asked about the signs and the man said, "Well, the water was going to waste, the bench was gathering dust in the attic, and the apple tree produced more than we could use. My wife and I thought it would be neighborly to offer tired, thirsty passersby a place to rest and refresh themselves. We've made a host of fine new friends!" he said.[40]

Look around you. Everyone has something to give! ✪

No one is useless in this world who lightens the burden of it to anyone else.

❂   ❂   ❂

Bear ye one another's burdens, and so fulfil the law of Christ.

Galatians 6:2 KJV

What do you do if you are diagnosed with a terminal disease and your family is too far away to help care for you? You might do what Susan Farrow did. She called together twelve of her close friends and said, "I need for you to be my family."

None of these friends was an expert in caring for the sick. Nonetheless, they dubbed themselves Susan's "funny family" and set out to help her the best they could. One baked brownies, another helped a daughter shop for clothes, another helped plan another daughter's wedding. One handled insurance paperwork, another organized medications, and one planned occasional entertainment.

Before Susan died in 1991, she told a friend that she believed she would have died three years earlier if it hadn't been for her friends. The friend agreed, "I think the energy of a group really does sustain a person."

Looking back, one of the "funny family" members said, "What I got out of the experience was learning how to take care of myself, to let other people in, to share the load. I got joy helping Susan."[41]

Part of your purpose in life is to care for others. Give the best you can, as often as you can.

A day hemmed in prayer is less likely to unravel.

✺　✺　✺

Do not worry about anything, but in everything by prayer and supplication with thanksgiving let your requests be made known to God. And the peace of God, which surpasses all understanding, will guard your hearts and your minds in Christ Jesus.

Philippians 4:6-7 NRSV

Mimi Rumpp believes her sister received a miracle. When she learned that her sister Miki was in need of a kidney transplant, Mimi prayed for a donor. Less than a year later Miki had a new kidney, courtesy of a woman who heard about her plight and had herself tested — she was a perfect match.

A rheumatoid arthritis patient participating in a scientific study on the effects of prayer said recently, "There's something weird going on here, and I love it." At the start of the experiment he had 49 tender joints. After four sessions of prayer by the laying-on-of-hands, he had only eight. Six months later he no longer needed pain medication.[42]

While skeptics may not attribute much power to prayer, a recent Newsweek survey revealed that 54 percent of American adults say they pray every day and 87 percent said they believe God answers their prayers at least some of the time. Some 86 percent said they accept God's failure to grant their prayers. Only 15 percent said they have lost faith — at any time — because their prayers went unanswered.

Even when public cynicism abounds, trust in God persists.

Have you made prayer a part of your day? ✪

Laziness travels so slowly, that poverty soon overtakes him.

He becometh poor that dealeth with a slack hand: but the hand of the diligent maketh rich.

Proverbs 10:4 KJV

One summer day, a man was driving on a lonely road. He came across a car with a flat tire. The car had been pulled over onto the shoulder of the road and a woman was standing next to it. She appeared greatly dismayed by her situation.

The man decided this was a good time to play the Good Samaritan. He pulled over and offered his services in helping her change the tire. She gratefully accepted.

The man grew hot and sweaty in the bright sun as he changed the tire. The lug nuts were difficult to loosen and his shirt was covered with tire marks and grease by the time he helped dig the jack and spare out of the trunk, wrangled the old tire off, and got the new tire securely mounted on the car.

The woman watched him with great appreciation and gave what encouragement she could. She thanked him repeatedly as he neared the end of the job, and then said, "Now, be sure and let the jack down easily. I don't want to awaken my husband. He's asleep in the back of the car."

Are you expecting others to do for you what you should be doing for yourself? Remember: *you* are the primary person responsible for *you*. As Robert Schuller has said: "If it's going to be, it's up to me." ✪

The journey of a thousand miles begins with a single step.

✿   ✿   ✿

By faith Abraham obeyed when he was called to set out for a place that he was to receive as an inheritance; and he set out, not knowing where he was going.

Hebrews 11:8 NRSV

One cent at a time. That is the approach taken by Common Cents, which now operates in 220 New York City schools. The students not only collect pennies, but also decide how to spend them.

The project is the idea of playwright Teddy Gross, who came up with the idea in 1989 after his three-year-old daughter Nora asked if they could take a beggar home. He says, "I wanted to encourage her concern, but I was at a loss for a way to take action. Then I remembered a neighbor who kept a cup of pennies that were just gathering dust." Soon Teddy and Nora were collecting pennies.

Gross took the idea of "harvesting pennies" to his synagogue and the congregation members raised $25,000. In 1992, the city invited Common Cents into the public schools and in three weeks, some 200,000 children raised nearly $100,000 for the victims of Hurricane Andrew.

In December 1996, the students contributed four-and-a-half tons of pennies, worth $16,000, to buy clothes for the homeless and food for a soup kitchen. In all, the group has given away more than $600,000 to more than 100 organizations. Collected one penny at a time.[43]

No amount is too little when given to God. ✪

You can never plan the future by the past.

Do not remember the former things, or consider the things of old. I am about to do a new thing.

Isaiah 43:18-19 NRSV

At age 23, Ken Benedict found himself serving a prison term for purchasing drug paraphernalia from an undercover cop. During his first months in prison, he fell into a deep depression, but gradually determined to turn his life around. He began attending services at the prison church and was assigned to work on the prison's computer. For his good behavior, he was assigned to work on an inmate crew that helped fight forest fires.

Fighting fires made Ken feel he was doing something positive. Little did he know he would be a hero the day in 1993 when fires swept through Malibu Canyon. Ken climbed a near vertical-face cliff, and then fought his way through thick smoke and large burning embers to rescue four members of a family who were fleeing from flames that were swirling some 70 feet high, pushing them down the cliff toward the ocean.

Later, Ken began to think, *If things hadn't gone the way they did, I wouldn't have been in a position to save their lives. Now maybe I can get on with my own.*

Following his release from prison the next year, Ken went to work for a computer company; two years later he was chosen Employee of the Year.[44]

God truly can work all things in your past for your future good. ✪

All our dreams can come true — if we have the courage to pursue them.

❂   ❂   ❂

*Be of good courage,
and he shall strengthen your heart,
all ye that hope in the LORD.*

Psalm 31:24 KJV

The team was leading 7 to 6 with only one minute left to play. The coach carefully instructed his quarterback not to pass under any condition. Even so, when the quarterback found himself within the opponent's ten-yard line, he was overcome by the temptation to pass for one more touchdown.

Unfortunately, as his coach had feared, the ball was intercepted — by the rival team's swiftest player. He broke into an open field and raced toward his goal. As he was speeding along, suddenly, out of nowhere, the quarterback who had thrown the intercepted pass overtook him and brought him down.

After the game, the losing coach remarked, "I'll never understand how your boy overtook my fastest player." The coach replied, "Your player was running for a touchdown — mine was running for his life!"

When we run in pursuit of our goals we, too, are "running for our lives" — the lives we were meant to live according to God's plan. Don't wait for others to motivate you, or to threaten you into action. Don't let yourself "throw away" your days by wasting them in idleness. Go for your highest and best. The goals you pursue are the only goals you will reach. ✸

None will improve your lot, if you yourselves do not.

❀   ❀   ❀

Do your best to improve your faith.
You can do this by adding goodness,
understanding, self-control, patience,
devotion to God,
concern for others, and love.

2 Peter 1:5-7 CEV

The children in the Barnstable Grade Five School have invented their own board game with handmade illustrations and rules they came up with themselves.

While this may sound like a "cute" school project, it has also proved to be one of the best fund-raising ventures the school has ever undertaken. The students netted $30,000 in sales in their first month, incorporated themselves as a business, hired lawyers, appointed a board of directors, and began production on a line of books, clothing, and videos. Their target? $1 million.

Carissa Souza, one of the young entrepreneurs, had this to say about the project, "We're going to have lots of money to go on field trips or get new things for the school, which is a great inspiration."

The Cape Cod community in which the school is located has attracted a large number of retirees without children, and the result in recent years has been a reluctance to increase spending for education. Prior to the project, even paper and pencils were in short supply. The annual budget for the school is $1.3 million, an amount the students are choosing to tackle as a goal, not view as a problem!

While none of us can ever earn the salvation of our souls, we each can do a great deal to earn our own way through life. ✪

The greatest achievements are those that benefit others.

❂　　❂　　❂

Do nothing from selfish ambition or conceit, but in humility regard others as better than yourselves. Let each of you look not to your own interests, but to the interests of others.

Philippians 2:3-4 NRSV

In his autobiography, Sir Edmund Hillary described the exhilaration of becoming the first to arrive at the peak of Mount Everest. At 11:45 AM on May 29, 1953, he and his guide, Norgay, stood on top of the world.

What most people don't know is that fifteen minutes after they arrived at the summit, the raw fury of nature forced them to begin their descent. Hillary recorded in his diary that unless they had begun the retreat back down the mountain immediately, nightfall would have overtaken them before they reached their base camp and they would have died. Their months of planning and weeks of hard climbing had given them only fifteen minutes of glorying in their success.[45]

When men pursue goals solely for selfish interests, they often find that their joy in accomplishment is very short-lived. Even more devastated, are those who find they have reached the top of their ladder only to discover that it was leaning against the wrong wall.

Perhaps it is time to retreat and refocus. Which mountain is it that God desires for you to climb? Of one thing you can be sure, when you reach the top of that mountain, you will arrive with others — both those who have helped you, and those whom you have helped. ✪

The ultimate measure of a man is not where he stands in moments of comfort and convenience, but where he stands at times of challenge and controversy.

✪   ✪   ✪

I have fought the good fight, I have finished the race, I have kept the faith.

2 Timothy 4:7 NKJV

*N*ational Geographic once ran a feature article about the Alaskan moose. The males of this species battle for dominance during the fall breeding season, literally going head-to-head, their antlers crunching together as they collide. In these collisions, their antlers are often broken.

When that happens, the moose with the broken antlers, his only weapon, knows that he is defeated. In the end, it is the heftiest moose, with the largest and strongest antlers, who triumphs.

The battle for supremacy is not really won, however, in these meadow clashes. It is actually won during the summer, when the moose eat continually, often nearly around the clock. The moose who consumes the best diet for growing antlers and gaining weight will be the heavyweight in the fall. Those who eat inadequately or incorrectly are the ones who will sport weaker antlers and less bulk and thus, fail.

For any of us to truly be able to run our race, to fight our fight of faith, or to stand and win against the assault of the enemy, we must prepare. Our ability to show courage in the face of challenge and controversy will be only as good as our discipline in preparation.

Feed your spirit today in God's Word and in prayer. Prepare yourself for life's inevitable battles. ✪

Give others a piece of your heart, not a piece of your mind.

❂   ❂   ❂

And be kind to one another,
tender-hearted, forgiving each other,
just as God in Christ also
has forgiven you.

Ephesians 4:32 NASB

During the first days of his presidency, while he and his family were still in their suite at the Willard Hotel in Washington, President Calvin Coolidge awoke early one morning to see a cat burglar going through his clothes. He watched him remove his wallet and a watch chain, at which point he said, "I wish you wouldn't take that . . . I don't mean the watch and chain, only the charm. Read what is engraved on the back of it."

The burglar read, "Presented to Calvin Coolidge, Speaker of the House, by the Massachusetts General Court." Coolidge then identified himself as the newly elected president, persuaded the burglar to relinquish the watch charm, and then led him into a quiet conversation.

He learned that the young man and his college roommate were unable to pay their hotel bill and buy train tickets back to their campus. Coolidge counted out $32 from his wallet to the dazed young man, declared it to be a loan, and advised the student to leave as unconventionally as he had entered to avoid the Secret Service.

Coolidge told only two friends about the incident, one of them Frank MacCarthy, who wrote about it fifteen years after Coolidge's death. According to MacCarthy, Coolidge said the young man repaid the loan in full.[46]

Mercy is sometimes more effective than justice. ✪

It's better to keep one's mouth shut and be thought a fool than to open it and resolve all doubt.

When words are many, sin is not absent, but he who holds his tongue is wise.

Proverbs 10:19

In 1872, George Westinghouse, inventor and manufacturer, applied for his first patent. It was for an automatic air brake that would function far more quickly and safely than the clumsy hand brakes in use at that time. The railroad companies were deeply suspicious of the invention, however. One of the skeptics was Cornelius Vanderbilt, president of the New York Central Railroad. When Westinghouse wrote to him pointing out the advantages of the air brake, Vanderbilt returned the letter with this message scrawled at the bottom: "I have no time to waste on fools."

Westinghouse next approached Alexander J. Cassatt of the Pennsylvania Railroad, who saw possibilities in the new brake and gave Westinghouse money to continue developing his invention. Tests on the brake were successful and word began to circulate among the railway industry that the invention would be available soon.

When this reached Vanderbilt, he wrote Westinghouse, inviting him to come and see him. Back came his letter, with a message from the inventor scrawled on the bottom, "I have no time to waste on fools. George Westinghouse."[47]

Many opinions are best left unvoiced. ✪

Plenty of people miss their share of happiness, not because they never found it, but because they didn't stop to enjoy it.

❂   ❂   ❂

Then will I go to the altar of God,
to God, my joy and my delight.
I will praise you with the harp,
O God, my God.

Psalm 43:4

Cineas was dismayed at the intent of Pyrrhus to undertake a war against the Romans. "Sir, when you have conquered them, what will you do next?" he asked.

"Sicily is near at hand and easy to master," said Pyrrhus.

"And what when you have conquered Sicily?"

"Then we will pass on to Africa and take Carthage," he replied.

"When these are conquered, what will be your next attempt?" asked Cineas.

"Then we will fall upon Greece and Macedon and recover what we have lost there."

"Well," pursued Cineas, "when all are subdued, what fruit do you expect from all your victories?"

"Ah," said Pyrrhus, "then we will sit down and enjoy ourselves."

"Sir!" said Cineas. "May we not do it now and forego all the preliminaries?"

Many times the ultimate happiness we are seeking is already at hand. We don't need to do anything further to earn it, achieve it, seek it, or conquer it. We only need to open our eyes and enjoy it.

In your pursuit of future blessings, don't fail to appreciate the blessings that God has already given you. ✪

We cannot be sure that we have something worth living for unless we are ready to die for it.

✦   ✦   ✦

If anyone would come after me, he must deny himself and take up his cross daily and follow me. For whoever wants to save his life will lose it, but whoever loses his life for me will save it.

Luke 9:23-24

Robert Chesebrough, the inventor of Vaseline, believed in his product. He was so convinced of its healing properties that he became his own guinea pig. He burned himself with acid and flame, and cut and scratched himself so often and so deeply, that he bore the scars of his tests for the rest of his life. But, in the process he proved that his product worked. People only had to look at his wounds, now healed, to see both the value of his work and the extent of his belief.

A medical scientist once took a similar approach. He so believed in a natural immune-boosting compound that he injected himself with several strains of an auto-immune disease in order to show his skeptical colleagues that his compound worked. He succeeded not only in healing himself, but in helping tens of thousands of others.

A surgeon took a similar risk. He was so convinced about the value of a certain anesthetic that he volunteered for a surgery using it so that others might see his example and be willing to undergo treatment.

When you put your life on the line for what you believe, what you believe can become a lifeline for others. ✪

We have to learn to be our own best friends because we fall too easily into the trap of being our own worst enemies.

✪ ✪ ✪

If I justify myself, mine own mouth shall condemn me: if I say, I am perfect, it shall also prove me perverse.

Job 9:20 KJV

In The Three Edwards, Thomas Costain tells of Raynald II, a fourteenth-century duke in what is now Belgium. After a bitter quarrel, Raynald's younger brother Edward led a revolt against him. Edward captured Raynald but did not kill him. Instead, he constructed a room for him in Nieuwkerk castle and promised him he could regain both his title and property as soon as he was able to leave the room. The room had several windows and a door of near-normal size, none of which were locked or barred.

The problem? Raynald's size. He often was called by his Latin nickname, Crassus, which means "fat." To regain his freedom, he had to lose weight! Edward, however, knew his older brother well and each day he sent him a variety of delicious foods. Instead of dieting his way out of his prison, Raynald grew fatter.

When Duke Edward was accused of cruelty, he had a ready answer: "My brother is not a prisoner. He may leave when he so wills." Raynald stayed in that room for ten years and wasn't released until after Edward died in battle. By then, he had ruined his health to the point that he died a year later.

Treat yourself today as you would treat God's most special creation. Indeed, you are! ✪

I don't know anything about luck.
I've never banked on it, and I'm afraid
of people who do. Luck to me is
something else; hard work and
realizing what is opportunity
and what isn't.

✿ ✿ ✿

He heard the sound of the trumpet, and
took not warning . . . But he that taketh
warning shall deliver his soul.

Ezekiel 33:5 KJV

John Sculley was very content in his job as an executive at Pepsico. Nevertheless, he agreed to meet with Steven Jobs, the young chairman of Apple Computer. Little did he know that Jobs had no intention of returning to California without convincing Sculley to go with him.

When Sculley and Jobs met in Sculley's penthouse office, Jobs asked what it would take for him to leave Pepsico.

"You'd have to give me a million-dollar salary, a million-dollar bonus, and a million-dollar severance," he replied.

Jobs was flabbergasted, but he agreed — if Sculley would move to California. Sculley only would agree to consulting from New York. At that, Jobs issued this challenge: "Do you want to spend the rest of your life selling sugared water, or do you want to change the world?"

Job's statement was a clarion-call to Sculley. He later admitted, "It knocked the wind out of me." He had become so caught up in his security at Pepsico that an opportunity to "change the world" nearly passed him by.

Do you recognize the opportunities God sends your way? They are what will make your day, and your life, full of meaning and purpose. ✪

I will not permit any man to narrow and degrade my soul by making me hate him.

✿   ✿   ✿

See that no one renders evil for evil to anyone, but always pursue what is good both for yourselves and for all.

1 Thessalonians 5:15 NKJV

Martin Luther King Jr. developed a ten-point rule of behavior to guide the nonviolent protests of the civil rights movement. His rules emphasized spiritual principles and inner attitudes, as well as specific practices. Every demonstrator agreed to:

l. Daily meditate on the teachings and life of Jesus.

2. Remember always that the nonviolent movement seeks justice and reconciliation, not victory.

3. Walk and talk in the manner of love, for God is love.

4. Pray daily to be used by God in order that all might be free.

5. Sacrifice personal wishes in order that all might be free.

6. Observe the ordinary rules of courtesy with both friend and foe.

7. Seek to perform regular service for others and the world.

8. Refrain from violence of fist, tongue, or heart.

9. Strive to be in good spiritual and bodily health.

10. Follow the directions of the movement and the captains of a demonstration.[48]

Even in the face of hate, an "up person" will live by the supreme law of love. When you are in a situation that requires you to exercise the rules of love, God will always give you the strength you need when you purpose to live by love. ✪

A man is not old until regrets take the place of dreams.

My days have passed, my plans are
shattered, and so are the
desires of my heart.

Job 17:11

A woman once told this story about a vacation she and her husband took in Hawaii. An organized and frugal man, her husband had reserved, well in advance, a compact car on each of the islands they planned to visit.

Upon arriving on the Big Island and presenting their reservation number, he was told that the economy car he had reserved was not available. Alarmed, the woman watched her husband's face flush bright red as he prepared to do battle. The clerk didn't seem to notice, however.

"Will you accept a substitute for the same price?" he asked. "We have a Mustang convertible." Only somewhat pacified, her husband agreed.

At the next island, they were again told their reserved car was unavailable and they were offered a same-price substitution. The same thing happened at the third and fourth stops. They ended up driving a Mazda MR-10, a Lincoln Town Car, and a Mercedes — all with sincere apologies and a compact-car rate.

On the plane home, the woman thanked her husband for such a memorable vacation. "Yes," he said, "it was really nice." Then, with all seriousness, he added, "But it was too bad they never had the right car for us."[49]

Don't regret shortcomings and errors to the point that you fail to appreciate God's blessings! ✪

**It is not the going out of port,
but the coming in that determines
the success of a voyage.**

✿   ✿   ✿

*One who puts on his armor should not
boast like one who takes it off.*

1 Kings 20:11

In *How Life Imitates the World Series*, Dave Bosewell tells a story about Baltimore Orioles' manager Earl Weaver and superstar Reggie Jackson.

Weaver had a rule that no one ever steal a base unless he was given the steal sign. Jackson felt he knew the pitchers and catchers well enough to judge for himself when he could steal, so one game he decided to steal without a sign. He got a good jump off the pitcher and easily beat the throw to second base. He felt great satisfaction! Weaver took Jackson aside and explained why he hadn't given the steal sign. The next batter up was power hitter Lee May. When Jackson stole second, first base was left open; the other team walked May intentionally, defusing the possibility for a hit.

The next batter had a poor record against the pitcher so Weaver sent in a pinch hitter to drive in the men on base, which decreased the team's bench strength. Jackson had to admit that he had seen an opportunity that only benefited him personally. Weaver, as manager, saw both the team and the game as a whole.

If we are to arrive victoriously in heaven's port, we are wise to take our signals from the One Who sees the big picture — all of humanity for all of eternity. He alone knows the ultimate game plan. ✪

Sometimes a winner is just a dreamer who never gave up.

✺   ✺   ✺

Because the Sovereign LORD helps me,
I will not be disgraced.
Therefore have I set my face like flint,
and I know I will not be put to shame.

Isaiah 50:7

According to the old tale, "The Flying Horse," a man who had been sentenced to death by the king begged a reprieve by attempting to strike a bargain: "I'll teach the king's horse to fly before a year goes by," the condemned man proclaimed. "If I don't succeed, you can take my life then."

The king was amused and granted the man's request.

"Are you crazy?" the man's friends asked him. "Why would you strike such a bargain? Surely you'll be dead by this time next year."

"A year is a long time," the man replied. "Much can happen in a year. Within a year the king may die. Or, I may die of other causes. Or perhaps the king's horse will die. Furthermore, who knows? Maybe the horse will learn to fly!"

A dreamer can always see multiple options for his future. He assumes that if one door closes, another door of equal value will open. One of the most important skills related to success is the ability to see many options, focus on those that are most beneficial, and then persist in pursuing them. ✪

Unless you enter the tiger's den you cannot take the cubs.

❈   ❈   ❈

How can anyone enter a strong man's house and carry off his possessions unless he first ties up the strong man?

Matthew 12:29

Deborah Major came face-to-face with the reality of her neighborhood's condition on the day her four-year-old son, Christopher, was attacked by a dog. The police seemed very slow to respond.

Major remembered the neighborhood as a place where "people took care of one another," but in the seven years she had been away, much had changed. Crack dealers, prostitutes, and gang members now ran the streets.

Deborah decided to take action. She invited her neighbors to attend a meeting to talk about their community's problems. Sixteen people showed up and by the end of the meeting they had a plan: They would take their concerns to city hall.

Major addressed the city council, but they took no action. When her home-grown group grew to fifty-eight home owners and four local businesses, the city finally began to listen. They increased building inspections and razed ten abandoned houses; efforts to exterminate rats increased. Neighbors began to help one another paint, patch, and clean up the area.

The mayor recently noted, "Thanks to one mother's outrage, a whole neighborhood has been swept with a new sense of pride."[50]

One person may not be able to win an entire battle single-handedly, but he can certainly lead the charge! ✪

Millions saw the apple fall, but Newton was the one who asked why.

✥ ✥ ✥

For I tell you that many prophets and kings desired to see what you see, but did not see it, and to hear what you hear, but did not hear it.

Luke 10:24 NRSV

By the early 1980s, no French cultural landmark was in greater need of renovation than the Louvre. The building had not been constructed as a museum and its layout was confusing. In fact, the Ministry of Finance had occupied nearly half of the building since the 1870s.

The Louvre hosted three million visitors annually — with only two bathrooms, a meager cafeteria, and a minimum of modern museum amenities. Only a very small fraction of the museum's collection could be displayed. Therefore, the Louvre had come to be called a "theater without a backstage" — having virtually no space for storage, conservation, research, or administrative services.

No one in France seemed concerned, however. Then one day the Minister of Culture, Jack Lang, took it upon himself to write a note to the newly elected President Mitterand asking him to consider creating a "Grand Louvre."

"It could be a beautiful symbol," Lang wrote. "Culture will win against finance." Mitterand was impressed, and the result was a complete and world-renowned remodeling.[51]

Is there a possibility that only you seem to see? Don't be afraid to give voice to your idea! ✪

When I look into the future, it's so bright it burns my eyes.

✿   ✿   ✿

I am like an olive tree flourishing in the house of God; I trust in God's unfailing love for ever and ever.

Psalm 52:8

When Abraham Lincoln was a boy he husked corn for three days to earn enough money to pay for a second-hand copy of the book, *The Life of Washington*. After he had read the book he announced, "I don't always intend to delve, grub, shuck corn, split rails, and the like."

"What do you want to be now?" asked Mrs. Crawford.

Lincoln confidently replied, "I'll be president."

Mrs. Crawford replied, "You'd make a purty president with all your tricks and jokes, now, wouldn't you?"

Abe responded with a confidence and wisdom far beyond his years or level of experience, "I'll study and get ready, and my chance will come."

And so it came to pass.

So many people are acclaimed as "overnight successes," when in fact, they have studied and prepared, honed their talents and skills, and gained valuable experience and wisdom — until their "chance" came.

No time spent in rehearsal or practice is ever wasted in God's economy. Everything we do is woven into His tapestry for our lives. Determine to spend a little time every day to develop your talents and learn new skills. Then when your chance comes, you'll be ready. ✪

Happiness is produced not so much by great pieces of good fortune that seldom happen, as by little advantages that occur every day.

✿ ✿ ✿

*Let us not grow weary while doing good,
for in due season we shall reap
if we do not lose heart.*

Galatians 6:9 NKJV

The afternoon had been filled with frenetic meetings and heated arguments. Everyone in the cast had frayed nerves and the heat of the day only served to increase the tension. Barbara Van Diest decided that when the cast broke for dinner, she'd drive home to change into more comfortable clothes and take a short breather in her cool, air-conditioned home.

As she drove out of the parking lot, her thoughts turned to Maria, who had been like a mother hen to all the cast members. She had been wonderful to each person, offering soothing words and kind pats on the back.

She deserves a rose, Barbara thought to herself. *I wish I had time to get one for her.* She knew, however, that she barely had time to get home, change, and get back before the meetings continued.

Then, as she stopped at a traffic light, a young man in the car next to hers rolled down his window and handed her a beautiful long-stemmed rose. The light changed and he was gone before she could even say thanks. So Barbara thanked God instead.[52]

God has blessings waiting around every corner today. Keep your eyes open. Take joy in those blessings and then pass blessings on to others. ✪

**To avoid criticism, do nothing,
say nothing, be nothing.**

✿   ✿   ✿

*Wisdom is too high for a fool; in the
assembly at the gate he has nothing to say.*

Proverbs 24:7

A Sunday school teacher was once telling the story of creation to her young students. She focused especially on the morning of the sixth day when God created all of the mammals. She went into great detail describing some of the unique characteristics of various creatures. Then she asked her students, "What's a foot or so long, has a bushy tail, climbs trees, and saves nuts?"

None of the young children offered an answer.

She repeated the question two more times, emphasizing the phrase "saves nuts."

After a long pause, one little boy finally mustered the courage to reply, "It sounds like a squirrel to me, but I'm sure the answer is supposed to be Jesus."

How many times do we think we have the right answer, a good idea, a workable solution, a sound opinion, or a fresh new approach that we feel confident will benefit all, yet we fail to speak up because we are afraid of criticism? The fact is, if we fail to speak up, something good fails to happen!

Take courage! Today, share what you know and believe, and above all, share the Christ in you. ❂

It took me a long time not to judge myself through someone else's eyes.

✪　✪　✪

Save me, O God, by thy name,
and judge me by thy strength.

Psalm 54:1 KJV

Baron von Welz, born to great wealth, gave up his title and his estates to live as a missionary in Dutch Guiana, where he died as an unheralded pauper.

As he gave up his title and prepared to depart for mission service, he said: "What to me is the title 'well-born' when I am born again in Christ? What to me is the title 'lord' when I desire to be a servant of Christ? What is it to me to be called 'Your Grace' when I have need of God's grace, help, and succor? All these vanities I do away with, and all else I will lay at the feet of Jesus, my dearest Lord, that I may have no hindrance in serving Him aright."

The opinion others have of you is never based on complete information — for who can truly know the deep secrets of your heart, your unspoken motives, or the beginning and ending of your life? In most cases, we are not even very good judges of ourselves.

The only eyes through which true judgment can come are the eyes of God. His eyes always are filled with love and mercy. And His judgment is aimed at correction, not condemnation. ✪

Men are born with two eyes but with one tongue, in order that they should see twice as much as they say.

❂   ❂   ❂

*For thy lovingkindness is before mine eyes:
and I have walked in thy truth.*

Psalm 26:3 KJV

A park ranger at Yellowstone National Park was leading a group of hikers to a fire lookout. The hikers were very interested in the plants and animals along the way, and the ranger was delighted to share his wealth of knowledge with them. He frequently stopped to describe various aspects of the beautiful nature through which they walked.

It seemed, however, that every time the ranger began to give an explanation, his two-way radio began to squawk. Each time he turned it down, and finally, in exasperation, he turned it off. The day was beautiful, no storm clouds in sight and no smoke on the horizon. What could possibly be of urgency?

Nearing the tower, he paused so the group could enjoy a particularly beautiful vista. He decided it was a good opportunity to check in with headquarters.

"Why haven't you responded to our messages?" they asked.

"Is something wrong?" the ranger replied.

"Yes! A grizzly bear was sited stalking your group, and we have been trying to warn you of the danger!"

Is there an important message coming your way today? Don't tune it out! ✣

The most wasted of all our days are those in which we have not laughed.

All the days of the afflicted are bad, but a cheerful heart has a continual feast.

Proverbs 15:15 NASB

In September 1862, President Abraham Lincoln called a special session of his closest advisers. When they arrived at the White House, they found him reading a book.

At first, Lincoln paid little attention to their entrance. Then, he started to read aloud to them a piece by the humorist Artemus Ward entitled "A High-Handed Outrage at Utica," which Lincoln found to be very funny.

At the end of his reading, Lincoln laughed heartily, but no one else joined in. The cabinet members sat in stony disapproval of the president's frivolity.

Lincoln rebuked them. "Why don't you laugh?" he asked. "With the fearful strain that is upon me night and day, if I did not laugh I should die, and you need this medicine as much as I do."

He then turned to business and told them that he had privately prepared "a little paper of much significance." It was the draft of the original Emancipation Proclamation.

The writer of Ecclesiastes tells us that there is a "time to weep and a time to laugh, a time to mourn and a time to dance" (Ecclesiastes 3:4). Life is intended to be neither all serious nor all frivolous. As in most things, balance is what counts. ✪

As long as you're green, you're growing; as soon as you're ripe you start to rot.

❂ ❂ ❂

They will still bear fruit in old age,
they will stay fresh and green.

Psalm 92:14

When she turned sixty-five, Mary Morrisey's mother informed her that she was starting a new club — the CMT club. "What does that stand for?" Mary asked.

"Can't Miss a Thing," her mother replied. "I don't want to live worrying about squeezing the last little drops out of my later years. I want to live them fully every moment. I'm going to practice not missing things I think I'm too old for." With that attitude, it was no surprise that Mary's mother chose to celebrate her seventy-fifth birthday by going skydiving.

Mary was amazed. After all, she had pins in her hip and a fragile pelvic bone from osteoporosis. When Mary asked her father how he felt about this ambition, he said, "I don't want anything to happen to your mother, but I'm not going to tell her she should narrow her life or limit her experiences because of fear. . . . I'm going to be at the airport to give her moral support."

Mary's mother trained for a tandem dive and then made four visits to the airfield before conditions were right for her skydiving experience. She called Mary after she had landed to say, "I did it! I did it! I was standing at the door of that airplane, twelve thousand feet in the air, and I stepped out. It's a symbol of my life now. I'm seventy-five and I'm stepping out!"[53] ✪

Acknowledgments

The publisher would like to thank the following for the quotes used in this book: Kay Lyons (8), Henry Kaiser (10), Dwight D. Eisenhower (12), Robert Schuller (14,34,90), Abraham Lincoln (16,76,150,184), Walt Disney (18,174), J.C. Penney (20), Charles Schwab (22), Albert Einstein (24), Dr. Michael Mantell (26), Eleanor Roosevelt (28), Zig Ziglar (30), Arnold Glasow (32,80,112), Dale Carnegie (36), Phillips Brooks (38), Lyn Karol (40), Italian Proverb (42), Jesuit Motto (44), Henry Ford (46), Isaac Singer (48), George Elliot (50), William James (52), Bill Cosby (54), Martin Luther King Jr. (56,124,180), Edwin Markham (58), Henry Emerson Fosdick (60), Dr. Wendell P. Loveless (62), Ben Stein (64), Ralph Waldo Emerson (66,142), Benjamin Franklin (68,104,120,168,208), James Baldwin (70), W. Clement Stone (72), Gill Robb Wilson (74), Cavett Robert (78), Peter Marshall (82), Aesop (84), Edmund Vance Cooke (86), Helen Keller (88), Reginald B. Mansell (92), Melba Colgrove (94), Will Rogers (96), George Bernard Shaw (98), English Proverb (100), Donna Reed (110), Earl Nightingale (116), James Openheim (118), Thomas Alva Edison (122,138), Alphonse Karr (126), Calvin Coolidge (128), Thomas Jefferson (130), Kate Halverson (132), Booker T. Washington (134,194), Winston Churchill (136), Doris Mortman (140), Corrie ten Boom (146), Vince Lombardi (148), Jean Kerr (150), Charron (152), William Jennings Bryan (156), Oscar Wilde (158) Sydney J. Harris (160), Leonard Nimoy (162), Charles Dickens (164), Edmund Burke (172), Bertolt Brecht (176), Denis Waitley (178), William Feather (186), Eric Hoffer (188), Roderick Thorpe (190), Lucille Ball (192), John Barrymore (196), Henry Ward Beecher (198), Japanese Proverb (202), Bernard Baruch (204), Oprah Winfrey (206), Elbert Hubbard (210), Sally Field (212), Charles Caleb Cotton (214), Sebastien Chamfort (216), Ray Kroc (218)

Endnotes

1 *Light from Many Lamps*, Lillian Eichler Watson, ed. (NY: Simon and Schuster, 1979), pp. 23-28.

2 Ibid., pp. 88-90.

3 *Reader's Digest*, July 1997, p. 33.

4 *Renaissance Lives*, Theodore Rabb (NY: Random House, 1993), pp. 23-31.

5 *Willard Scott's Down Home Stories*, Willard Scott (NY: Bobbs-Merrill Co., 1984), pp. 129-130.

6 Ibid., pp. 130-131.

7 *Everyone Is Entitled to My Opinion*, David Brinkley (NY: Alfred A. Knopf, 1996), p. 114.

8 Tulsa World, August 5, 1996, pp. 1-2.

9 *M.D.*, B.H. Kean, M.D. (NY: Ballantine Books, 1990), pp. 14-15.

10 *Runner's World*, May 1996, pp. 93-94.

11 *Out of the Blue*, Mark Victor Hansen and Barbara Nichols (NY: Harper Collins, 1996), pp. 109-110.

12 *San Luis Obispo County Telegram-Tribune*, June 5, 1997, A-5.

13 *Willard Scott's Down Home Stories*, Willard Scott (NY: Bobbs-Merrill Co., 1984), p. 21.

14 *When Smart People Fail*, Carole Hyatt and Linda Gottlieb (NY: Simon and Schuster, 1987), pp. 36-37.

15 *Union Life*, November/December 1994, p. 24.

16 *Out of the Blue*, Mark Victor Hansen and Barbara Nichols (NY: Harper Collins, 1996), pp. 69-70.

17 Ibid., pp. 52-53.

18 *Everyone Is Entitled to My Opinion*, David Brinkley (NY: Alfred A. Knopf, 1996), p. 126.

19 *A Moment in the Day*, Mary Beckwith and Kathi Mills (Ventura, CA: Regal Books, 1988), pp. 243-244.

20 *Reader's Digest*, December 1996, pp. 145-146.

21 *Guideposts*, December 1996, pp. 58-59.

22 *Success*, March 1997, p. 8.

23 *Light from Many Lamps*, Lillian Eichler Watson, ed. (NY: Simon and Schuster, 1979), pp. 142-145.

24 *Success*, January/February 1997, pp. 31-32.

25 *Walking with Christ in the Details of Life*, Patrick Morley (Nashville: Thomas Nelson, 1992), pp. 9-10.

26 *Jesus CEO*, Laurie Beth Jones (NY: Hyperion, 1995), pp. 207-208.

27 *Reader's Digest*, May 1997, pp. 74-79.